DEPARTMENT OF JUSTICE
TAX DIVISION

SUMMONS ENFORCEMENT MANUAL

An Introduction

Co-Authors:

Frank P. Cihlar

Rachel D. Cramer

Frank de Leon

Deborah S. Meland

Ann Carroll Reid

Norma J. Schrock

May 2006

TABLE OF CONTENTS

May 2006

TABLE OF AUTHORITIES

CASES   **PAGE(S)**

STATUTES:

MISCELLANEOUS:

I. INTRODUCTION

Section 7602 of the Internal Revenue Code (I.R.C.)(26 U.S.C.) authorizes the IRS to "examine any books, paper, records or other data" that may be relevant to determine or collect the amount of tax, penalties, and interest owed to the Government by any taxpayer. In the vast majority of investigations, the taxpayer or third party voluntarily produces information to the IRS. This may come in response to an IRS form known as an Information Document Request (IDR), a letter from the Service, or just in the course of a conversation between an IRS agent or officer and a taxpayer or third party.

In the event the person who has the information refuses to provide it voluntarily or if the Service for whatever reason decides not to make an informal request and chooses to proceed more formally, Congress has given the IRS the power to issue an administrative summons in order to compel a taxpayer or a third party to produce the information   in the form of documents or testimony or both   for use in its investigation. The summons will describe the information requested and the investigation to which the IRS thinks that information may be relevant. The summons will also specify where and when the information must be produced. If the summoned party does not comply, the IRS must decide whether it wishes to pursue the matter. If it does, the Service must ask the Department of Justice to obtain a court order enforcing the summons. If the court orders enforcement and the summoned party still refuses to produce the summoned information, the refusal may result in sanctions for civil or criminal contempt.

As an attorney for the Department of Justice, one of the most important things for you to remember when you receive a summons enforcement case is that the summoned information is important to an ongoing investigation. Because the summons enforcement process, even when expedited, tends to be time-consuming, it is unlikely that an agent or revenue officer would ask for enforcement unless they really need the information to complete their work. In most cases, the statute of limitations on making assessments, collecting the taxes, or making a decision to bring a criminal case will still be running while your summons enforcement case is pending. All of this means that for summons enforcement to be a valuable tool, cases must be brought and pursued on an expedited basis. It is our hope that the information in this Manual will help you litigate the cases knowledgeably and expeditiously.

II. LAW

A. IRS SUMMONS AUTHORITY

The United States' system of taxation relies on self-assessment and the good faith and integrity of each taxpayer to disclose completely and honestly all information relevant to his tax liability. Nonetheless, "it would be naive to ignore the reality that some persons attempt to outwit the system." *United States v. Bisceglia*, 420 U.S. 141, 145 (1975). Thus, Congress has charged the Secretary of the Treasury and the Commissioner of Internal Revenue with the responsibility of administering and enforcing the Internal Revenue Code. *See* I.R.C. §§ 7601 and 7602; *Madison v. United States*, 758 F.2d 573, 574 (11th Cir. 1985).

To this end, Section 7601 of the Code directs the Secretary to make inquiries into the tax liability of every person who may be liable to pay any internal revenue tax. *Codner v. United States*, 17 F.3d 1331, 1332 (10th Cir. 1994). In turn, Section 7602 authorizes the Secretary to examine books, papers, records, or other data, to issue summonses, and to take testimony for the purpose of: (1) "ascertaining the correctness of any return," (2) "making a return where none has been made," (3) "determining the liability of any person for any internal revenue tax . . . ," (4) "collecting any such liability," or (5) "inquiring into any offense connected with the administration or enforcement of the internal revenue laws." *See, e.g., United States v. Euge*, 444 U.S. 707, 710-11 (1980); *United States v. LaSalle Nat'l Bank*, 437 U.S. 298, 308 (1978); *United States v. Rockwell Int'l*, 897 F.2d 1255, 1261 (3d Cir. 1990).

The summons statutes, I.R.C. §§ 7602-7613, provide the IRS with an investigative device that is to be interpreted broadly in favor of the IRS. *See Euge*, 444 U.S. at 714-15 (holding that the language of § 7602 includes authority to summons some physical evidence, and upholding a summons for handwriting exemplars). Congress's intent was to foster effective tax investigations by giving the IRS expansive information-gathering authority. *See United States v. Arthur Young & Co.*, 465 U.S. 805, 816 (1984) (citing *Bisceglia*, 420 U.S. at 146); *United States v. Norwest Corp.*, 116 F.3d 1227, 1231-32 (8th Cir. 1997). Restrictions on the summons power are to be avoided, absent unambiguous Congressional direction. *See Arthur Young*, 465 U.S. at 816; *Euge*, 444 U.S. at 715. *See also United States v. Stuart*, 489 U.S. 353, 364 (1989); *Robert v. United States*, 364 F.3d 988, 996 (8th Cir. 2004). The Supreme Court has cautioned against restricting the summons authority absent express legislative direction. *See Tiffany Fine Arts, Inc. v. United States*, 469 U.S. 310, 318 (1985); *United States v. Barter Sys., Inc.*, 694 F.2d 163, 167 (8th Cir. 1982); *United States v. Clement*, 668 F.2d 1010, 1013 (8th Cir. 1982).

Once a summons is issued, however, it is not self-enforcing. If the person to whom a summons is issued fails to comply, the Government must seek judicial enforcement under I.R.C. §§ 7402(b) and 7604(a).[1] These sections confer authority upon the United States district courts to issue orders compelling compliance with an Internal Revenue Service summons. Because the enforcement of a summons invokes the process of the court, a court will not enforce a summons if enforcement would constitute an abuse of that process. *United States v. Powell*, 379 U.S. 48, 58 (1964); *Rockwell Int'l*, 897 F.2d at 1261.

B. JUDICIAL REVIEW OF A SUMMONS

The validity of an IRS summons may come before a district court in one of two ways. First, because a summons is not self-enforcing, the Government may bring an enforcement proceeding seeking a court order directing compliance with the summons. (*See* Section II(B)(3).) Second, in the case of a third-party summons, certain persons may be entitled to bring a proceeding to quash the summons. (*See* Section II(B)(4).) Under no circumstance,

---

[1] If the summoned party's refusal is willful, he may also be prosecuted under I.R.C. § 7210. *See United States v. Becker*, 259 F.2d 869 (2d Cir. 1958) (affirming a conviction for violating Section 7210, where the defendant had willfully and knowingly neglected to produce certain of the books and papers called for under a summons issued by an IRS special agent); *see also, Reisman v. Caplin*, 375 U.S. 440, 446 (1964) ("any person summoned who 'neglects to appear or to produce' may be prosecuted under § 7210"). Similarly, if the summoned party wholly makes default or contumaciously refuses to comply, he may be subject to sanctions under I.R.C. § 7604(b), including arrest and punishment for contempt. *See Reisman*, 375 U.S. at 448. Indeed, when a Section 7604(b) complaint is filed, "[i]f the taxpayer has contumaciously refused to comply with the administrative summons and the Service fears he may flee the jurisdiction, application for the sanctions available under § 7604(b) might be made simultaneously with the filing of the complaint." *United States v. Powell*, 379 U.S. 48, 58 n.18 (1964). *But see Schulz v. IRS*, 395 F.3d 463, *reh'g granted*, 413 F.3d 304 (2d Cir. 2005) (without citing or discussing *Becker*, holding that a summoned party cannot be held in contempt or subjected to indictment under Section 7210 absent an enforcement order.)

however, is a summoned party entitled to bring a proceeding to quash the summons. (*Id.*)

1. Burdens of production and persuasion

However a summons proceeding is initiated, the standard and burden of proof is the same. In either case, the Government bears the ultimate burden of persuasion. S. Rep. No. 97-494, vol. 1, at 283 (1982), *reprinted in* 1982 U.S.C.C.A.N. 781, 1029 ("[a]lthough an action to quash the summons must be instituted by the taxpayer, the ultimate burden of persuasion with respect to its right to enforcement of the summons will remain on the Secretary, as under current law"); *see Crystal v. United States*, 172 F.3d 1141, 1143-44 (9th Cir. 1999) (stating that the Government must make the same showing whether to "defeat a petition to quash, or to enforce a summons").

The Government has the initial burden of making a prima facie showing that the summons is valid. (*See Section II(B)(2).*) But the Government's burden is "a slight one" that can be satisfied by a declaration from the investigating agent. *Crystal*, 172 F.3d at 1144; *United States v. Garden State Nat'l Bank*, 607 F.2d 61, 68 (3d Cir. 1979); *Alphin v. United States*, 809 F.2d 236, 238 (4th Cir. 1987); *2121 Arlington Heights Corp. v. IRS*, 109 F.3d 1221, 1224 (7th Cir. 1997); ; *United States v. Balanced Fin. Mgmt., Inc.*, 769 F.2d 1440, 1443 (10th Cir. 1985); *In re Newton*, 718 F.2d 1015, 1019 (11th Cir. 1983).

Once the Government makes its prima facie case, the opposing party has a heavy burden to show that enforcement would be an "abuse of process." *Fortney v. United States*, 59 F.3d 117, 120 (9th Cir. 1995). To carry this burden the challenger must show more than mere legal conclusions, and must allege specific facts and evidence to support his allegations. *Garden State Nat'l Bank*, 607 F.2d at 68; *Liberty Fin. Servs. v. United States*, 778 F.2d 1390, 1393 (9th Cir. 1985).

2. Requirements for a valid summons

The validity of a summons is measured by standards established both by the Supreme Court and by Congress.

a. The Supreme Court's *Powell* requirements

The Supreme Court established the framework for judicial review of a summons in *United States v. Powell*, 379 U.S. 48 (1964). In that case the Court held that the IRS did not have to satisfy any standard of probable cause in order to issue a valid summons. All that the Government must show is that the summons (1) is issued for a legitimate purpose; (2) seeks information that may be relevant to that purpose; (3) seeks information that is not already within the IRS's possession; and (4) satisfies all administrative steps required by the Internal Revenue Code. *Powell*, 379 U.S. at 57-58.

(1) The summons was issued for a legitimate purpose

Congress has given the IRS broad directions under Section 7601 to investigate "all persons . . . who may be liable" for taxes. Sections 7602(a) and (b) delineate the purposes for which an IRS summons may be issued:

- Ascertaining the correctness of any return,
- Making a return were none has been made,
- Determining the liability of any person for any internal revenue tax or the liability at law or in equity of any transferee or fiduciary of any person in respect of any internal revenue tax,
- Collecting any such liability, or
- Inquiring into any offense connected with the administration or enforcement of the internal revenue laws.

In *Powell*, the Supreme Court thus noted that the IRS can issue a summons to investigate "'merely on suspicion that the law is being violated, or even just because it wants assurance that it is not.'" 379 U.S. at 57 (quoting *United States v. Morton Salt Co.*, 338 U.S. 632, 642-43 (1950)).

When the Supreme Court later held that a summons could not be issued in aid of a criminal investigation, *United States v. LaSalle Nat'l Bank,* 437 U.S. 298 (1978), Congress enacted Section 7602(b) permitting the use of summons to gather information in aid of a criminal investigation. *See Scotty's Contracting & Stone, Inc. v. United States*, 326 F.3d 785 (6th Cir. 2003). Section 7602(d), however, prohibits the issuance or the enforcement of a summons with respect to a person if there is in effect a "Justice Department referral" as defined in the statute. *(See Section II(B)(2)(b).)*

(2) The summoned information may be relevant

Section 7602 authorizes the IRS to examine "any books, papers, records, or other data which *may* be relevant or material." (Emphasis added.) In *United States v. Arthur Young & Co.*, 465 U.S. 805, 814 (1984), the Court stated that the language "may be" reflects Congress's express intention to allow the IRS to obtain "items of even *potential* relevance to an ongoing investigation, without reference to its admissibility." (Emphasis in original.) The IRS need not show that the "documents it seeks are actually relevant in any technical, evidentiary sense." *Arthur Young*, 465 U.S. at 814. In *Powell*, the Supreme Court noted that the IRS can issue a summons to investigate "'merely on suspicion that the law is being violated, or even just because it wants assurance that it is not.'" 379 U.S. at 57 (quoting *Morton Salt*, 338 U.S. 642-43). Thus, in applying the *Powell* test, the question is not whether the records sought, when disclosed, will contradict a taxpayer's return, but whether the records "might" throw light upon the correctness of a return. *Arthur Young*, 465 U.S. at 814-15 & n.11. The IRS need not accept the word of the summoned party that records are not relevant. It is entitled to determine that fact for itself. *See Tiffany Fine Arts, Inc. v. United States*, 469 U.S. 310, 323 (1985).

Relevancy determinations necessarily are factual and normally are reviewed on appeal only for clear error. *United States v. Goldman*, 637 F.2d 664, 667 (9th Cir. 1980). Relying on the Supreme Court's pronouncements in *Arthur Young*, the various courts of appeals have had little trouble in construing the *Powell* relevance standard broadly.

- *Sylvestre v. United States*, 978 F.2d 25, 27 (1st Cir. 1992) (records of taxpayer's savings accounts, checking accounts, and the like are relevant to purpose of determining possible income tax liability).

- *PAA Mgmt., Ltd. v. United States,* 962 F.2d 212, 217-18 (2d Cir. 1992) (IRS may seek enforcement of summons even after issuance of statutory notice of deficiency because Tax Court could redetermine the correct amount of the deficiency).

- *United States v. White*, 853 F.2d 107, 116-17 (2d Cir. 1988) (summons for records of attorney/executor of estate enforced as having "potential" relevance to determination whether fees were deductible under state law).

- *United States v. Rockwell Int'l*, 897 F.2d 1255, 1263 (3d Cir. 1990) (liberal standard of relevance to be applied to determine whether material in "free reserve file" is relevant to investigation of correctness of corporation's 1983 tax return).

- *Barquero v. United States*, 18 F.3d 1311, 1318 (5th Cir. 1994) (IRS may summon records for time-barred years so long as those records are relevant to later years under investigation).

- *United States v. El Paso Co.*, 682 F.2d 530, 537 (5th Cir. 1982), (taxpayer's "tax-pool analysis" documents that focus on questionable positions in the tax return are highly relevant even though they were not used in preparing the tax return).

- *United States v. Abrahams*, 905 F.2d 1276, 1279 n.1, 1281 (9th Cir. 1990) (summons to attorney for "all documents relating to preparation of income tax returns for others" enforced since such documents were likely to "throw light" on clients' tax returns) *overruled on other grounds by United States v. Jose,* 131 F.3d 1325, 1329 (9th Cir. 1997) (en banc).

- *United States v. Giordano*, 419 F.2d 564, 568 (8th Cir. 1969) (holding that the Commissioner is "licensed to fish"). *But see United States v. Dauphin Deposit Trust Co.*, 385 F.2d 129, 131 (3d Cir. 1968) (IRS "is not entitled to go on a fishing expedition . . . . [but] must identify with some precision the documents it wishes to inspect").

The relevancy test for a summons is a relatively low one, but it is not non-existent. The Government must establish that there is some realistic expectation (more than an idle hope) that the summoned information may be relevant to its investigation. Although the summoned documents or information need not meet the evidentiary relevancy requirement for admissibility, the Government should show some logical connection between the information sought and the purpose of the exam. In most cases, the potential relevance of the summoned information is self-evident. In other instances, an explanation may be helpful.

- *United States v. Matras*, 487 F.2d 1271, 1275 (8th Cir. 1973) (A corporation not required to produce copies of its budgets when the IRS justified its request on the need for a "roadmap" to better understand the corporation's operations. "The term 'relevant'

7

connotes and encompasses more than 'convenience.' . . . If we were to accede to the government's view, it is difficult to imagine corporate materials that might not contribute to a more comprehensive understanding of the workings of the corporation, and thus, according to the government, be deemed relevant to the tax investigation.").

- *David H. Tedder & Assocs. v. United States*, 77 F.3d 1166, 1169 (9th Cir. 1996) (names of a law firm's clients need not be revealed when the IRS did not demonstrate that the specific client identities "might throw light upon the correctness" of the taxpayer's return).

- *United States v. Monumental Life Ins. Co.*, 440 F.3d 729 (6th Cir. 2006) ("The present case exemplifies an exceptional circumstance where automatic reliance upon an agent's affidavit is not adequate because (1) the subpoena is directed to a third party, not to the taxpayer being investigated, (2) the IRS seeks a voluminous amount of highly sensitive propriety information about Monumental's general administration of its products, (3) the IRS has opposed the imposition of a protective order, and (4) the magistrate judge, who spent years considering the scope of the summons, found that the IRS was seeking 'some irrelevant information.'")

The results in these cases thus might have been different if the potential relevance of the summoned information had been better described.

(3) The summoned information is not already in the possession of the IRS

To satisfy the third *Powell* requirement, the IRS must show that the summoned information is not already in the IRS's possession. As noted above, the simple statement in the IRS agent's declaration that the summoned information is not in the possession of the IRS is sufficient to shift the burden of proof to the party opposing enforcement to come forward with evidence to the contrary. This *Powell* requirement may not be satisfied, however, when someone in the IRS other than the declaring agent has the summoned information and it is available for use in the exam.

The courts have "declined to apply a literal interpretation of this *Powell* criterion in favor of a practical approach to IRS accessibility." *United States v.*

John G. Mutschler & Assocs., Inc., 734 F.2d 363, 367-68 (8th Cir. 1984). The Fifth Circuit explained this "practical approach" as follows:

> The "already possessed by government" defense originated in the passage of *United States v. Powell* [ ], for which the Supreme Court cited no authority. *Powell* construed not only the implicit prerequisites to enforceability of a summons issued under 26 U.S.C. §§ 7602, 7604(b), but also the explicit limitation contained in 26 U.S.C. § 7605(b), which forbids "unnecessary" summonses. Read in context, we construe the "already possessed" principle enunciated by *Powell* as a gloss on § 7605(b)'s prohibition of "unnecessary" summonses, rather than an absolute prohibition against the enforcement of any summons to the extent that it requests the production of information already in the possession of the IRS.

United States v. Davis, 636 F.2d 1028, 1037 (5th Cir. 1981). *But see United States v. Monumental Life Ins. Co.*, 440 F.3d 729 (6th Cir. 2006) (rejecting claim that documents obtained by IRS in the course of investigating another taxpayer were not accessible because of the confidentiality provisions of I.R.C. § 6103(a)).

The following are instances where the courts have applied the practical approach to IRS accessibility.

- **Difficult to retrieve** - *United States v. First Nat'l State Bank*, 616 F.2d 668, 673-74 (3d Cir. 1980) (the IRS can summon documents that may be in its possession but which are difficult to retrieve). *See also United States v. Linsteadt*, 724 F.2d 480, 484 (5th Cir. 1984); *cf. United States v. Theodore*, 479 F.2d 749, 755 (4th Cir. 1973) (court refused to enforce a summons directed to a tax preparer for copies of all the returns of his clients for three years because there was no record evidence that the IRS could not readily retrieve the information).

- **Different versions** - *United States v. Davey*, 543 F.2d 996, 1001 (2d Cir. 1976) (may demand production of original documents rather than copies); *United States v. Luther*, 481 F.2d 429, 432 (9th Cir. 1973) (access to records from other sources "does not destroy the government's right to inspect the original and primary records of the Corporation"); *United States v. Daffin*, 653 F.2d 121, 124 (4th Cir.

1981) (retained copies of tax returns to compare with the originals filed with the IRS).

- **Second look** - *Spell v. United States*, 907 F.2d 36, 38 (4th Cir. 1990) (taxpayer may not refuse to comply with summons issued by special agent merely because his returns were examined previously by revenue agent); *United States v. Lang*, 792 F.2d 1235, 1242 (4th Cir. 1986) (allowing a "second look" for a different and additional purpose); *United States v. Morgan*, 761 F.2d 1009, 1011 (4th Cir. 1985) (special agent's fraud inquiry is considered a continuation of the original, uncompleted audit); *United States v. Popkin*, 623 F.2d 108, 109 (9th Cir. 1980) (per curiam) (examination by revenue agent does not "fulfill the needs of a special agent investigating fraud"); *United States v. Lenon*, 579 F.2d 420, 422 (7th Cir. 1978) (fraud investigation "different in both approach and extent" from a routine audit); *United States v. Garrett*, 571 F.2d 1323, 1328-29 (5th Cir. 1978) (IRS's entitlement to a single meaningful examination may necessitate additional scrutiny of documents by the special agent).

(4) The summons meets all administrative requirements

The fourth element of the *Powell* test is that the IRS comply with the administrative steps required by the Code. These steps include service on the summoned party and, in the case of a third-party summons, notice to any person identified in the summons.

Courts occasionally have excused minor failures to comply with the required administrative steps provided that the taxpayer has not been prejudiced thereby. *United States v. Texas Heart Inst.*, 755 F.2d 469, 478 (5th Cir. 1985) (provided that the taxpayer has had *"every benefit* of the administrative steps required by the Code, a failure by the IRS to meet the technical niceties of the statute will not bar enforcement") (emphasis in original), *overruled on other grounds, United States v. Barrett*, 837 F.2d 1341 (5th Cir. 1988); *United States v. Privitera*, 75 A.F.T.R.2d (RIA) 1266, 1266 (9th Cir. 1995) ("Minor violations will be excused where the IRS acts in good faith and there is no prejudice to the taxpayer."). But even though the Sixth Circuit allowed enforcement of a summons despite a nonprejudicial administrative deficiency, it cautioned that it expected the IRS to strictly adhere to all administrative niceties in future cases. *See Cook v. United States*, 104 F.3d 886 (6th Cir. 1997). In other words, "technical" violations should be not treated lightly.

- **Service on the summoned party** - Section 7603 specifies how a summons should be served on the summoned party. Part (a) provides the general method of service "by an attested copy delivered in hand to the person to whom it is directed, or left at his last and usual place of abode." An attested copy is merely a copy of the original summons with an signed statement on its face that it is a true and accurate copy. *Mimick v. United States*, 952 F.2d 230 (8th Cir. 1991). Part (b) provides that summonses issued to "third-party recordkeepers," as that term is defined in Section 7603(b)(2), may be served "by certified or registered mail to the last known address" of the summoned party. I.R.C. § 7603(b)(1) "Third-party recordkeepers" include banks, financial institutions, credit card companies, attorneys, and accountants. The mandates of Rule 4 of the Federal Rules of Civil Procedure do not apply to the service of IRS summonses. *United States v. Gilleran*, 992 F.2d 232, 233 (9th Cir. 1993); *United States v. Bichara*, 826 F.2d 1037, 1039 (11th Cir. 1987). Section 7603(a) also provides that "a certificate of service signed by the person serving the summons shall be evidence of the facts it states on the hearing of an application for the enforcement of the summons."

- **Notice to others of a third-party summons** - Section 7609(a)(1) requires that a person identified in a summons receive notice if the summons seeks information "with respect to" that person. The most obvious case is when a third party (*i.e.,* bank) is summoned to produce records relating to a taxpayer's examination. In that case the taxpayer must receive notice of the summons. The less obvious case is when a third party is summoned to produce another person's records (*i.e.,* parent's, girlfriend's) in connection with a taxpayer's examination. Any other person whose records are identified in the summons should receive notice.

   Section 7609(a) also establishes the method of such notice, which can be provided in person or by certified or registered mail. It must be served within three days after the summons is served and at least 23 days before the summons compliance date. The notice must include a copy of the summons and an explanation of that person's right to bring a proceeding to quash the summons. Several courts have held that the notice copy need not include the attestation required of the copy served on the summoned party. *Codner v. United States*, 17 F.3d 1331, 1333-34 (10th Cir. 1994); *Fortney v. United States*, 59 F.3d 117, 120-21 (9th Cir. 1995). In *United States v. Mimick*, 952 F.2d at 231-32, however, the

Eighth Circuit held that attested copies must be served on both the summoned party and any noticee.

- **Notice to taxpayer of third-party contact** - Section 7602(c), added to the Code as part of the Internal Revenue Service Restructuring and Reform Act of 1998, Pub. L. No. 105-206, § 3417(a), 112 Stat. 685, 757-58, provides that "[a]n officer or employee of the Internal Revenue Service may not contact any person other than the taxpayer with respect to the determination or collection of the tax liability of such taxpayer without providing reasonable notice in advance to the taxpayer that contacts with persons other than the taxpayer may be made." Failure to notify taxpayer of a third-party contact is a serious defect. In *United States v. Jillson*, 84 A.F.T.R.2d (RIA) 99-7115 (S.D. Fla. 1999), the court denied enforcement of summonses to third parties because the IRS had not issued a notice of contact to the taxpayer prior to issuing the summonses.

b. No "Justice Department referral" is in effect - § 7602(d)

In addition to satisfying the *Powell* requirements, a summons must also satisfy a specific statutory requirement. In *LaSalle Nat'l Bank,* 437 U.S. 298 (1978), the Supreme Court held that a summons could not be issued in aid of a criminal investigation. Congress responded four years later by enacting Section 7602(b), which permits the use of a summons to gather information in aid of a criminal investigation. Tax Equity and Fiscal Responsibility Act of 1982 (TEFRA), Pub. L. No. 97-248, § 333(a), 96 Stat. 324, 621-22. Section 7602(d), however, enacted at the same time, precludes either the issuance of a summons or the commencement of a proceeding to enforce it once a "Justice Department referral" is in effect with respect to the person whose liabilities are under investigation. The phrase "Justice Department referral" is a term of art and embraces the following:

A Justice Department referral is in effect with respect to any person if --

(i) the Secretary has recommended to the Attorney General a grand jury investigation of, or the criminal prosecution of, such person for any offense connected with the administration or enforcement of the internal revenue laws, or

(ii) any request is made under section 6103(h)(3)(B) for the disclosure of any return or return information (within the meaning of section 6103(b)) relating to such person.

I.R.C. § 7602(d)(2)(A).

Each taxable period and each tax imposed by a separate IRC chapter are treated separately. I.R.C. § 7602(d)(3). Thus, a summons issued with respect to the examination of the 1979 and 1980 years was proper, despite an indictment alleging tax crimes for 1976 and 1977. *Commissioner v. Hayes*, 631 F. Supp. 785, 787 (N.D. Cal. 1985). *See also United States v. Pittman*, 82 F.3d 152, 157 (7th Cir. 1996) (offenses related to taxes from different chapters of the IRC or offenses under different titles, such as Title 26 (taxes) and Title 31 (money laundering) are treated separately).

In general, courts have recognized that Section 7602(d) created a bright line, with a "Justice Department referral" being the line of demarcation. *See Scotty's Contracting & Stone,* 326 F.3d 785 (collecting cases). But the law in the Fourth and Seventh Circuits is not entirely clear. *United States v. Berg*, 20 F.3d 304, 309 n.6 (7th Cir. 1994) (noting that the IRS "cannot use its summons authority if its only purpose is to gather evidence for a criminal investigation, (i.e. if it has "'no civil purpose whatsoever' and [it] 'has abandoned any institutional pursuit of civil tax determination.'") (citations omitted). *Compare Hintze v. IRS*, 879 F.2d 121, 127 (4th Cir. 1989) (stating that the summons may have been quashed if the taxpayers had shown "that the IRS was pursuing its investigation for the sole purpose of building a case on anticipated criminal charges"), *overruled on other grounds, Church of Scientology v. United States*, 506 U.S. 9, 15 n.8 (1992), *with Morgan*, 761 F.2d at 1012 (stating that Section 7602(d) "drew a 'bright line' indicating that the summons power ended at the point where an investigation was referred to the Justice Department for prosecution" (citations omitted)). In the Fourth and Seventh Circuits, it is important that the agent's declaration clearly state that the IRS has not abandoned its civil purpose. Thus, for example, when a summons is issued by a Special Agent in aid of a criminal investigation, the declaration should indicate that any related civil liabilities, which may include penalties, have not been finally determined and the information sought is relevant to that determination as well.

The IRS may not issue a summons or seek to enforce it if the IRS already has made an institutional decision to make a "Department of Justice referral." Such conduct would constitute bad faith. *United States v. Jose*, 131 F.3d 1325, 1328 (9th Cir. 1997) (en banc) ("It is well established that the IRS is acting in bad faith if it pursues a summons enforcement after having already decided to make a recommendation for prosecution . . . .") (citing

LaSalle Nat'l Bank, 437 U.S. at 317 and *United States v. Stuart*, 489 U.S. 353, 362 (1989)).

c. Requirements to summon certain subject matters

Special procedures apply to summonses seeking information concerning certain subjects.

(1) Cable Communications Policy Act

The Service takes the position that it must comply with Section 631 the Cable Communications Policy Act of 1984,[2] 47 U.S.C. § 551, when issuing a summons to a cable company. Chief Counsel Advisory, IRS CCA 200230034, 2002 WL 1730123. Section 551(c)(1) generally prohibits a cable company from disclosing a subscriber's "personally identifiable information," without the prior written or electronic consent of the subscriber concerned. "Personally identifiable information" "does not include any record of aggregate data which does not identify particular persons." 47 U.S.C. § 551(a)(2)(A).[3]

If the cable company provides either internet or telephone service in addition to cable television service, however, disclosure of the information relevant to the internet or telephone service is *not* restricted by Section 551 of the Cable Act. Disclosure of information relevant to internet or telephone service is permitted under Section 2703(c)(2) of the Electronic Communications Privacy Act, 18 U.S.C., and Section 551(c)(2)(D) of the Cable Act. *See In re Application of the United States of Am. for an Order Directed to Cablevision Sys. Corp.*, 158 F. Supp. 2d 644 (D. Md. 2001).

---

[2] Pub. L. No. 98-549, 98 Stat. 2779.

[3] The Senate report states that "[t]he phrase 'to collect personally identifiable information' covers the various ways that individuals can be identified, including name, address, and social security number." S. Rep. No. 98-67, at 28 (1984). The cognate House report, paraphrasing the statute, states that "'personally identifiable information' . . . would include specific information about the subscriber, or a list of names and addresses on which the subscriber is included, but does not include aggregate information about subscribers which does not identify particular persons." H.R. Rep. No. 98-934, at 79 (1984), *reprinted in* 1984 U.S.C.C.A.N 4655, 4716.

Where Section 551 of the Cable Act applies, it is subject to several exceptions, including one that permits disclosure in response to a court order obtained by a governmental entity.[4] 47 U.S.C. § 551(c)(2)(B). Such an order, however, (1) must be based on clear and convincing evidence that the subscriber is reasonably suspected of having engaged in criminal activity and that the information sought would be material evidence in the case, and (2) must be obtained in a proceeding in which the subscriber is afforded the opportunity to appear and contest the claim. 47 U.S.C. § 551(h). *See United States v. Cox Cable Communications*, 81 A.F.T.R.2d (RIA) 2011 (N.D. Fla. 1998) (holding the IRS satisfied the requirements of Section 551(h) with the agent's declaration).

(2) *Health Insurance Portability and Accountability Act (HIPAA)*

When the IRS requests health information protected by the Health Insurance Portability and Accountability Act (HIPAA) of 1996 Privacy Regulations, 45 C.F.R. parts 160 and 164, from a "covered entity" (*e.g.*, a physician, healthcare organization, health insurer, etc.), it may have additional burdens to meet in order to secure the information. "Protected health information" is defined, *inter alia*, as information, in any form, maintained by a covered entity that can identify the individual and relates to that individual's health, receipt of healthcare services, or the past, present, or future payment for the healthcare services provided. *See* 45 C.F.R. § 160.103. Additionally, documents containing information that would identify the healthcare recipient's relatives, employers, or household members can also qualify as protected information. 45 C.F.R. § 164.514(b).

Three exceptions allow the Service to obtain protected health information while enforcing the Internal Revenue Code: the consent of the taxpayer, the law enforcement exception, and the administrative and judicial proceedings exception. Chief Counsel Notice CC-2004-034, addresses the standards for applying those exceptions. IRS CCN CC-2004-034, 2004 WL 3210766.

---

[4] Exceptions are also made if the disclosure is necessary to render (or conduct a legitimate business activity related to) a service to the subscriber (Section 551(c)(2)(A)), the disclosure is of the subscriber's name and address to any cable or other service, provided certain conditions are satisfied (Section 551(c)(2)(C)), or the disclosure is to a government entity as authorized under chapters 119, 121, or 206 of Title 18, provided the disclosure does not reveal the subscriber's selection of video programming (Section 551(c)(2)(D)).

An administrative summons issued under Section 7602(a)(2) qualifies under the law enforcement exception. In addition to the usual requirements for enforcement, however, a summons seeking protected health information must satisfy a three-pronged test: (1) the information sought must be "relevant and material" to a "legitimate law enforcement inquiry"; (2) the request must be "specific and limited in scope to the extent reasonably practicable in light of the purpose for which the information is sought"; and (3) "[d]e-identified information could not reasonably be used." 45 C.F.R. § 164.512(f)(1)(ii)(C). The privacy rules list eighteen specific identifiers, ranging from traditional categories such as name and address to less traditional categories such as web addresses, biometric identifiers (*e.g.*, finger and voice prints), account numbers, and vehicle identification numbers (*e.g.*, license plates).

To satisfy the requirements of the three-pronged test, the Service is to supplement any summons for protected health information with a statement that the three additional requirements have been met. CC-2004-034, *4. A covered entity may reasonably rely on such a statement and produce the summoned information. 45 C.F.R. § 164.514(h)(2). A declaration accompanying a request to bring a summons enforcement action should incorporate the requirements of the three-pronged test and represent that they have been satisfied.

(3) Tax accrual workpapers

Special rules apply when issuing and seeking enforcement of a summons issued for tax accrual workpapers. Enforcement of such summonses should be handled by the Tax Division. As a matter of practice, the Deputy Assistant Attorney General (Civil Trial Matters) and the appropriate Section Chief should be notified whenever a suit to enforce a summons for tax accrual workpapers has been received by the Tax Division.

Tax accrual workpapers are documents and memoranda relating to an auditor's evaluation of a taxpayer's reserves for contingent tax liabilities. Such workpapers may contain information pertaining to the taxpayer's financial transactions, identify questionable positions taken on tax returns, and reflect the auditor's opinions regarding the validity of such positions. *United States v. Arthur Young & Co.,* 465 U.S. 805 (1984); United States v. El Paso Co., 682 F.2d 530, 533-35 (5th Cir. 1982). Tax accrual workpapers are generally prepared as a part of the process of auditing a corporation's financial statements, not as part of the tax return preparation process. The tax accrual workpapers can be prepared by in-house or outside accountants.

In *Arthur Young,* the Supreme Court rejected the argument that the workpapers were privileged. A summons for tax accrual workpapers is enforceable so long as the documents meet the low threshold of relevance and the other *Powell* requirements for enforcement.

The IRS, however, has adopted a policy of restraint in seeking tax accrual workpapers. Announcement 2002-63, 2002-2 C.B. 72; I.R.M. 4.10.20. Consequently, there is little case law on this subject, and even after *Arthur Young,* courts may entertain assertions of work-product and other privileges. *See, e.g., United States v. Rockwell Int'l*, 897 F.2d 1255 (3d Cir. 1990) (reversing the enforcement of a summons seeking tax accrual workpapers when the district court failed to also consider whether the documents were protected by the attorney-client privilege).

3.   Enforcement actions

If the summoned party fails to comply with the summons, Section 7604 provides the United States with a means to enforce the summons by filing an enforcement proceeding in federal district court. *(See,* Section III.A.)

a.   No conditional enforcement

There is no authority for a court to conditionally enforce a summons. *United States v. Jose*, 131 F.3d 1325 (9th Cir. 1997) (en banc); *United States v. Barrett*, 837 F.2d 1341, 1350-51 (5th Cir. 1988) (en banc) (per curiam).[5] The power of the court in a summons enforcement case is "'strictly limited to granting or denying enforcement of the terms of the specific summons.'" *United States v. Abrahams*, 905 F.2d 1276, 1287 (9th Cir. 1990) (quoting *United States v. First Nat'l State Bank*, 540 F.2d 619, 624-25 (3d Cir. 1976)).

---

[5] In *United States v. Zolin*, 491 U.S. 554 , 561(1989), the Supreme Court found itself "evenly divided with respect to the issue of the power of a district court to place restrictions upon the dissemination by the IRS of information obtained through a § 7604 subpoena action" and therefore affirmed the judgment of the Court of Appeals for the Ninth Circuit, insofar as it upheld the district court's conditional-enforcement order. Such an affirmance is not binding in other cases, *see Hertz v. Woodman*, 218 U.S. 205, 213-14 (1910), and the Ninth Circuit later reversed its *Zolin* decision in *Jose*, 131 F.3d at 1329.

Nothing in the Internal Revenue Code authorizes a court to engraft "equitable" requirements on its enforcement order so as to limit the IRS's internal use of the summoned information. *See Reisman v. Caplin*, 375 U.S. 440 (1964) (injunction issued against IRS summons dismissed for want of equity); *United States v. First Family Mortgage Corp.*, 739 F.2d 1275, 1278 (7th Cir. 1984) (Tax Anti-Injunction Act barred taxpayer's request for an injunction against IRS's use of summoned information). Although the summons power is not absolute, restrictions on that authority should not be imposed "'absent unambiguous directions from Congress.'" *United States v. Arthur Young & Co.*, 465 U.S. 805, 816 (1984) (quoting *United States v. Bisceglia*, 420 U.S. 141, 150 (1975)).

b. Withdrawal and reissuance

It is always the IRS's prerogative to withdraw a summons it has issued; and in most cases, if not all, it is free to reissue the summons. In the case where a procedural defect is detected, consider whether withdrawal and reissuance would be appropriate. Some courts have overlooked technical defects in the issuance of a summons where the taxpayer or summoned party has not suffered prejudice. *United States v. Texas Heart Inst.*, 755 F.2d 469 (5th Cir. 1985), *overruled on other grounds by United States v. Barrett,* 837 F.2d 1341 (5th Cir.1988) (en banc) (per curiam); *Sylvestre v. United States*, 978 F.2d 25, 27-28 (1st Cir. 1992); *United States v. Bank of Moulton*, 614 F.2d 1063, 1066 (5th Cir. 1980). But not all courts do it lightly. In *Cook v. United States*, 104 F.3d 886 (6th Cir. 1997), the IRS had provided the taxpayers with just 22 days notice of the compliance date for a third-party summons, instead of the 23 days mandated by Section 7609(a)(1). The Sixth Circuit affirmed the denial of the taxpayers' petition to quash, as taxpayers conceded that they had suffered no actual prejudice from the violation, but cautioned that its decision should not be taken as "a license to ignore statutory deadlines or to negligently violate other legal requirements" and that the "court shall review future violations of technical legal requirements by the I.R.S. and its agents and attorneys with an increasingly critical eye." 104 F.3d at 890-91.

When an IRS summons is withdrawn, a petition to quash that summons becomes moot. *Malone v. Humphrey*, 237 F.2d 55 (6th Cir. 1956); *Gillings v. United States*, 95 A.F.T.R.2d (RIA) 1014 (9th Cir. 2005); *Pintel v. United States*, 74 A.F.T.R.2d (RIA) 5105 (C.D. Cal. 1994). *Dame v. United States*, 643 F. Supp. 533, 534 (S.D.N.Y. 1986); *Kearns v. United States*, 580 F. Supp. 8, 10 (S.D. Ohio 1983); *Pac. Fisheries, Inc. v. United States*, 94 A.F.T.R.2d (RIA)

5953 (W.D. Wash. 2004); *Dollar v. United States*, 57 A.F.T.R.2d (RIA) 998 (W.D. Wash. 1985).

c. Effect of taxpayer appeal

(1) Order is enforceable unless stayed

In the absence of a stay pending appeal, once a district court orders a summons enforced, the summoned party must comply with the court's order, notwithstanding the taking of an appeal. On occasion, taxpayers have contended that they were entitled to a stay of a summons enforcement order under Fed. R. Civ. P. 62(d), which provides that a stay may be obtained "by giving a supersedeas bond."[6] But a stay under Rule 62(d) is "subject to the exceptions contained in subdivision (a) of [the] rule." Rule 62(a) provides an automatic 10-day stay of execution upon a judgment or of proceedings for its enforcement, but excepts from its scope "an interlocutory or final judgment in an action for an injunction" and directs that the discretionary provisions of subdivision (c) "govern the suspending, modifying, restoring, or granting of an injunction during the pendency of an appeal." The automatic stay provisions of Rule 62(a) and (d) are thus most often, if not always, confined to cases involving money judgments. *See, e.g., Hebert v. Exxon Corp.*, 953 F.2d 936, 938 (5th Cir. 1992) ("Courts have restricted the application of Rule 62(d)'s automatic stay to judgments for money because a bond may not adequately compensate a non-appealing party for loss as a result of the stay of a non-money judgment."). We know of no case holding that a summons enforcement order was subject to an automatic stay.

A party, however, may seek a discretionary stay of an enforcement order pending appeal, as it might any other order or judgment. *See* Fed. R. Civ. P. 62 and Fed. R. App. P. 8. Ordinarily, the party seeking a stay must first move for a stay in the district court. Fed. R. App. P. 8(a)(1). A motion for a stay may be made to the court of appeals, if the movant can show that moving

---

[6] In *Becker v. United States*, 451 U.S. 1306 (1981), the taxpayers offered to post a supersedeas bond and argued they were entitled under Rule 62(d) to a stay of an IRS summons enforcement order pending appeal to the Ninth Circuit. Chief Justice Rehnquist, acting as Circuit Justice, issued an order in which he granted a temporary stay in order to allow the full Court to consider the issue of Rule 62(d)'s availability. But the full Court did not take up the issue and the stay was lifted. *See* 452 U.S. 935.

first in the district court would be impracticable or can state that the district court has denied the movant's request for a stay. Fed. R. App. P. 8(a)(2)(A).

The standards for determining whether a stay pending appeal should be granted require that the moving party establish: (i) a "strong" showing that it will prevail on the merits on appeal; (ii) that irreparable injury will result unless the stay is granted; (iii) that issuance of a stay will result in no substantial harm to other interested persons; and (iv) that issuance of a stay will result in no substantial harm to the public interest. *Hilton v. Braunskill*, 481 U.S. 770, 776 (1987); *Adams v. Walker,* 488 F.2d 1064, 1065 (7th Cir. 1973). If the movant fails to establish that he satisfies all four requirements, he will not be entitled to a stay.

Courts are not likely to grant a stay pending appeal of a summons enforcement order.

> A stay pending appeal from [an order enforcing] a summons should not be granted as a matter of course, but only when there is a substantial possibility of success, and then on terms designed to expedite the appeal and, if necessary and appropriate, to protect against the running of any applicable statute of limitations.

In re Turner, 309 F.2d 69, 72 (2d Cir. 1962) (cited in *Multistate Tax Comm'n v. United States Steel Corp.*, 659 F.2d 931, 932 (9th Cir. 1981)).

(i) *Likelihood of success on the merits*   Given the IRS's broad investigative power and the highly deferential clear error standard of review, *see, e.g., United States v. Claes*, 747 F.2d 491, 495-96 (8th Cir. 1984), once the district court has determined that the *Powell* requirements have been satisfied, the movant usually has little, if any, likelihood of overturning a summons enforcement order on appeal. After all, Section 7602 gives the IRS broad, although not unlimited, power to investigate. It extends the summons power to the examination of "any books, papers, records, or other data which *may be relevant* or material" to an inquiry. I.R.C. § 7602(a) (emphasis added). "The language 'may be' reflects Congress' express intention to allow the IRS to obtain items of even *potential* relevance to an ongoing investigation, without reference to its admissibility." *Arthur Young*, 465 U.S. at 814 (emphasis in original). On that ground alone, a stay should usually be denied. But the other requirements are equally formidable.

(ii) *Irreparable injury in the absence of a stay*   Historically, a movant might have argued he would be irreparably injured if a stay were not granted, because compliance with the summons would moot his appeal from the enforcement order. However, this argument has been taken away. In *Church of Scientology v. United States*, 506 U.S. 9 (1992), the Supreme Court held that compliance with IRS summonses did not moot an appeal from an enforcement order issued by a district court because "if the summons were improperly issued or enforced a court could order that the IRS's copies of the tapes be either returned or destroyed." 506 U.S. at 15.

So, too, any alleged damage to the movant's business or reputation caused by compliance with a summons enforcement order does not constitute irreparable harm as a matter of law. *See Acierno v. New Castle County*, 40 F.3d 645, 653 (3d Cir. 1994) (preliminary injunction case: "[e]conomic loss does not constitute irreparable harm"); *Morton v. Beyer*, 822 F.2d 364, 371 (3d Cir. 1987) (preliminary injunction case: "we do not believe that loss of income alone constitutes irreparable harm").

(iii - iv) *The balance of hardships and the public interest*
Because the Government is always a party to the summons enforcement proceeding, the third and fourth criteria for granting a stay under *Hilton v. Braunskill,* 481 U.S. at 776, namely, that issuance of a stay will result in no substantial harm to other interested persons and will result in no substantial harm to the public interest, merge into one. *See Washington Metro. Area Transit Comm'n v. Holiday Tours, Inc.*, 559 F.2d 841, 843 (D.C. Cir. 1977) ("[t]he interest of the Commission and of the riding public is largely the same as that of the general public"). In that regard, the public's interest in the efficient and even-handed administration of the revenue laws is never served by a stay. It has long been recognized that the Government needs "to assess and collect taxes as expeditiously as possible with a minimum of preenforcement judicial interference." *Bob Jones Univ. v. Simon*, 416 U.S. 725, 736 (1974). The information provided by a summons plays an important role in the process of enforcing the tax laws. When a summons is not complied with promptly, the Government must take a detour from the orderly road of its investigation. These delays hamper the progress of enforcement and contravene the public interest. *Cf. United States v. Kis*, 658 F.2d 526, 540 (7th Cir. 1981) (noting "Congress's concern that summons enforcement proceedings be concluded rapidly"). The public's interest in vigorous and thorough enforcement of the revenue laws should thus always weigh heavily against granting a stay.

(2) Compliance does not moot an appeal

"It has long been settled that a federal court has no authority 'to give opinions upon moot questions or abstract propositions, or to declare principles or rules of law which cannot affect the matter in issue in the case before it'. . . . For that reason, if an event occurs while a case is pending on appeal that makes it impossible for the court to grant 'any effectual relief whatever' to a prevailing party, the appeal must be dismissed." *Church of Scientology*, 506 U.S. at 12 (quoting *Mills v. Green*, 159 U.S. 651, 653 (1895)). Relying on these principles, the Government used to contend that compliance with a summons mooted an appeal of the district court's enforcement order. But that is no longer true.

In *Church of Scientology*, the Government acquired possession of two summoned tape recordings, after the District Court ordered enforcement of the summons, but while the enforcement order was on appeal. Relying on the authority of the majority (eight of nine) of the Circuit Courts of Appeal that had considered the issue, the Government moved to dismiss the appeal on the ground of mootness. The Ninth Circuit agreed and dismissed the appeal. The Supreme Court granted certiorari to consider the issue. Instead of relying on the line of cases cited by the Government involving IRS summonses, the Court chose instead to rely on numerous decisions holding that compliance with a district court order enforcing a Federal Trade Commission subpoena did not moot an appeal of the enforcement order. Consequently, the Supreme Court held that compliance with an order enforcing an IRS summons did *not* moot an appeal of the enforcement order, because "if the summons were improperly issued or enforced a court could order that the IRS's copies of the [summoned material] be either returned or destroyed." 506 U.S. at 15.

Although *Church of Scientology* was a loss for the Government, it is not without benefit. If nothing else, it precludes a losing party from contending that it should be entitled to a stay pending appeal on the ground that compliance with the summons enforcement order would result in the irreparable harm of mooting the appeal.

c. Remedies for failure to obey enforcement order

If a party ordered to comply with an IRS summons does not obey that order, the Government may move by way of contempt proceedings to compel compliance. *See, e.g., United States v. Brown*, 918 F.2d 82 (9th Cir. 1990); *United States v. Riewe*, 676 F.2d 418, 421 (10th Cir. 1982). District courts have inherent power to enforce compliance with orders through contempt. *Shillitani v. United States*, 384 U.S. 364, 370 (1966).

Contempt of court is defined in Blacks Law Dictionary as conduct that defies the authority or dignity of a court. A motion for contempt in federal court, whether civil or criminal, is premised on 18 U.S.C. § 401(3), which provides that "[a] court of the United States shall have power to punish by fine or imprisonment, or both, at its discretion, such contempt of its authority, and none other, as . . . [d]isobedience or resistance to its lawful writ, process, order, rule, decree, or command."

In contrast to criminal contempt, civil contempt is designed to force the contemnor to comply with an order of the court. *Int'l Union, United Mine Workers v. Bagwell*, 512 U.S. 821 (1994). A district court may impose a sanction for contempt only if it finds that the party requesting the sanction has proven contempt by clear and convincing evidence. *Peterson v. Highland Music, Inc.*, 140 F.3d 1313, 1323 (9th Cir. 1998); *Chicago Truck Drivers v. Bhd. Labor Leasing*, 207 F.3d 500, 505 (8th Cir. 2000).

For a party to be held in contempt, it must be shown that: (1) a valid order existed, (2) the party had knowledge of the order, and (3) the party disobeyed the order. *Reliance Ins. Co. v. Mast Constr. Co.*, 159 F.3d 1311, 1315 (10th Cir. 1998). The moving party is required only to establish a prima facie case of contempt by demonstrating that certain conduct was required by a previous court order and that the alleged contemnor failed to comply with that order. *United States v. Hayes*, 722 F.2d 723, 725 (11th Cir. 1984). A prima facie case for contempt may be made either by affidavits attached to the petition, or by sworn testimony presented in open court. The show cause order places on the alleged contemnor the burden of showing why he should not be held in contempt. *United States v. Rylander*, 460 U.S. 752, 757 (1983). The defendant must present some evidence to explain or justify his failure to produce the requested information. *McPhaul v. United States*, 364 U.S. 372, 379 (1960); *Morrison v. California*, 291 U.S. 82, 88-89 (1934).

The only question at the contempt stage is whether the contemnor has the present ability to obey the court's enforcement order. In raising this defense, the defendant bears the burden of production. *Rylander*, 460 U.S. at 757. The defendant does not meet this burden simply by alleging nonpossession of the summoned documents and asserting a Fifth Amendment privilege. *Rylander*, 460 U.S. at 758-62, *United States v. Rue*, 819 F.2d 1488 (8th Cir. 1987).

Any questions regarding the propriety of the summons and whether it should have been enforced must have been raised in the enforcement hearing. *Rylander*, 460 U.S. at 757. "[The] contempt proceeding does not open to reconsideration the legal or factual basis of the order alleged to have been disobeyed and thus become a retrial of the original controversy." *Maggio v. Zeitz*, 333 U.S. 56, 69 (1948).

In the contempt proceeding the summoned party must be able to show that he or she had made all reasonable efforts to comply with the summons to avoid contempt. *See United States v. Seetapun*, 750 F.2d 601, 605-06 (7th Cir. 1984); *Hayes*, 722 F.2d at 725-26. A defendant "demonstrates [an] inability to comply [with a court order] only by showing that he has made 'in good faith all reasonable efforts to comply.'" *United States v. Roberts*, 858 F.2d 698, 701 (11th Cir. 1988) (citation omitted) (affirming contempt where contemnor's record searches did not amount to "all reasonable efforts").

In *United States v. Hayes*, 722 F.2d 723, Hayes, a summoned tax promoter, partially complied with an order enforcing the summons, but claimed that some of the documents were being held in Switzerland by Hayes's business partner, who refused to release them. Despite Hayes's alleged "diligent requests" involving trips to Switzerland to obtain the documents, the appellate court found that Hayes failed to make "all reasonable efforts" to comply with the order: "[O]ther avenues for obtaining the material were never explored." Hayes failed to take any actions against his business partner, including researching his legal rights, threatening his business partner with legal action, or consulting an attorney. "He cannot carry his burden... merely by adducing evidence that he has *requested* the documents, when it appears that he has greater leverage at his disposal." 722 F.2d at 725-26 (emphasis in original).

Because such contumacious conduct interferes with the administration of justice, it is punishable by coercive sanctions to induce compliance, or by remedial sanctions to compensate an aggrieved party for losses sustained for past disobedience of the court's order. *Feltner v. Title Search Co.*, 283 F.3d 838, 841 (7th Cir. 2002). In fashioning sanctions for civil contempt, district courts should consider "the character and magnitude of the harm threatened by continued contumacy, and the probable effectiveness of any suggested sanction in bringing about the result desired." *United States v. United Mine Workers*, 330 U.S. 258, 304 (1947). Appropriate sanctions may include a coercive daily fine, a compensatory fine, or coercive incarceration. *Int'l Union*, 512 U.S. 821; *United States v. Marquardo*, 149 F.3d 36 (1st Cir. 1998);

O'Connor v. Midwest Pipe Fabrications, Inc., 972 F.2d 1204, 1211 (10th Cir. 1992).

(1) Coercive Fines

When fixing the amount of coercive daily fines, district courts must also consider "the amount of defendant's financial resources and the consequent seriousness of the burden to that particular defendant." *United Mine Workers*, 330 U.S. at 304. One appellate court upheld fines of $5,000 a day for failure to turn over documents pursuant to a summons enforcement order. *United States v. Darwin Constr. Co.*, 873 F.2d 750 (4th Cir. 1989). Coercive fines may exceed the $1,000 criminal fine under Section 7210 for failure to comply with a summons. *United States v. Hefti*, 879 F.2d 311, 315 (8th Cir. 1989).

(2) Coercive Imprisonment

The basis for permitting a court summarily to order coercive imprisonment for recalcitrant persons without affording them the safeguards of a criminal proceeding is that the contemnors hold "the keys of the prison in their own pockets," and therefore can purge themselves of the contempt at any time. *In re Nevitt*, 117 F. 448, 461 (8th Cir. 1902). When a court finds that confinement has lost its coercive effect, it essentially becomes punitive and the contemnor must be released. *See, e.g.*, *Lambert v. Montana*, 545 F.2d 87 (9th Cir. 1976); *In re Grand Jury Investigation (Braun)*, 600 F.2d 420, 423-24 (3d Cir. 1979); *Simkin v. United States*, 715 F.2d 34, 36-37 (2d Cir. 1983). To hold the contemnor longer would violate due process. *Lambert*, 545 F.2d at 89.

Although the due process test is easily formulated (*i.e.*, when incarceration no longer has a coercive effect, it violates due process), the point at which coercive imprisonment ceases to be coercive and essentially becomes punitive is not readily discernible. While the courts have not formulated a bright-line test to determine whether a contemnor has met his burden of persuasion, it is well settled that a person's insistence that he will never comply is not sufficient. *Lambert*, 545 F.2d at 90 (citing *Catena v. Seidl*, 343 A.2d 744, 747 (N.J. 1975)). "Obviously, the civil contempt power would be completely eviscerated were a defiant witness able to secure his release merely by boldly asserting that he will never comply with the court's order." *Braun*, 600 F.2d at 425. What has emerged, therefore, is the requirement that the contemnor bear the burden of establishing that there is no substantial likelihood that continued confinement would accomplish its coercive purpose. *Id.* (citing *Lambert*, 545 F.2d at 90-91). Self-serving statements about present intention not to comply is not persuasive evidence that the defendants will not change their minds. *See Simkin*, 715 F.2d at 37 (a contemnor's present intention not to comply does not preclude the possibility that continued confinement will cause a change of mind).

A court must make an individualized decision whether there remains a realistic possibility that continued confinement might cause the contemnor to comply. *In re Crededio*, 759 F.2d 589, 592 (7th Cir. 1985). In making its decision, a court should be mindful that incarceration of contemnors for civil contempt is premised on the notion that the desire for freedom, and concomitantly the willingness to comply, increases with the time spent in prison. *Braun*, 600 F.2d at 428; *In re Martin-Trigona*, 590 F. Supp. 87, 91 (D. Conn. 1984). Courts have not hesitated to incarcerate civil contemnors for periods greater than a year. *See, e.g., United States v. Lippitt*, 180 F.3d 873, 878 (7th Cir. 1999) (finding incarceration remains coercive after two years); *CFTC v. Armstrong*, 284 F.3d 404, 408 (2d Cir. 2002) (upholding continued civil contempt incarceration after period of more than two years); *In re Lawrence*, 279 F.3d 1294 (11th Cir. 2002) (over two years); *Chadwick v. Janecka*, 312 F.3d 597 (3d Cir. 2002) (holding no constitutional ban to incarcerating defendants seven years where defendant has present ability to comply with order).

(3) *Compensatory Fines*

Compensatory fines compensate the party for injuries resulting from the contemptuous behavior. *Gen. Signal Corp. v. Donallco, Inc.*, 787 F.2d 1376, 1380 (9th Cir. 1986). The amount of compensatory sanctions includes the actual costs incurred by the moving party. *Id.* Compensatory damages may also include the amount of loss sustained by the contumacy. *United States v. Berg*, 20 F.3d 304, 311 (7th Cir. 1994). *See also Connolly v. J.T. Ventures*, 851 F.2d 930, 932 (7th Cir. 1988) (holding that the loss due to contempt in a copyright infringement action may include profits from the sale of the items).

Actual costs incurred by the moving party include attorneys fees and costs of attending the contempt hearing. A reasonable hourly rate to award for fees is the amount "according to the prevailing market rates in the relevant community." *Schwarz v. Sec'y of Health & Human Servs.*, 73 F.3d 895, 906 (9th Cir. 1995) (citing *Blum v. Stenson*, 465 U.S. 886, 895 (1984)); *see also United States v. City of Jackson*, 359 F.3d 727, 733 (5th Cir. 2004) ("When a court awards attorney's fees to the government as a sanction for an adverse party's improper conduct, [ ] we treat the hourly rate in the local legal community as a benchmark for determining the amount of attorney's fees to be imposed."); *United States v. Big D Enters., Inc.*, 184 F.3d 924, 936 (8th Cir. 1999) (same); *Napier v. Thirty or More Unidentified Fed. Agents*, 855 F.2d 1080, 1093 (3d Cir. 1988) (same). The Government may argue that, at a minimum, the Government should be awarded a rate equal to the rate referenced in the Equal Access to Justice Act (28 U.S.C. § 2412(d)(2)(A), effective 1996). *See City of Jackson*, 359 F.3d at 734. The statutes allows for adjustments for inflation. The Bureau of Labor Statistics' Consumer Price Index inflation calculator is listed at the following website: http://www.bls.gov/cpi/home.htm. *See Am. Wrecking Corp. v. Sec'y of Labor*, 364 F.3d 321, 330 (D.C. Cir. 2004).

4.   Petitions to quash third-party summons

Certain persons are entitled to bring a judicial proceeding to quash a summons. A summoned party, whether or not the taxpayer under investigation, is *never* entitled to commence an action to contest the validity of an IRS summons. If he has a good faith reason to refuse compliance, his only recourse is to wait and defend an enforcement action brought against him by the Government. It is only the case of a summons issued to a third party that offers an opportunity for a pre-enforcement challenge, but even then, not by the summoned third party. If, under Section 7609(a), notice of a third-party summons is required to be given to any person (including the taxpayer) identified in the summons, the person receiving such notice (the "noticee") is entitled, under Section 7609(b)(2) to bring a proceeding to quash the summons. But certain requirements must be met.

a.   Requirements

Section 7609 sets forth several requirements relating to time of filing, requirement of notice, and location of the suit. The requirements are jurisdictional: they comprise part of the conditions of the United States' waiver of sovereign immunity and must be strictly adhered to by the petitioner. *Berman v. United States*, 264 F.3d 16, 19 (1st Cir. 2001) (motion to quash must be filed within 20 days of mailing notice); *accord Faber v. United States*, 921 F.2d 1118 (10th Cir. 1990); *Stringer v. United States*, 776 F.2d 274 (11th Cir. 1985); *Ponsford v. United States*, 771 F.2d 1305, 1309 (9th Cir. 1985). As sovereign immunity cannot be waived unless the statutory conditions have been met, counsel for the United States have no authority to disregard or overlook failures to comply with the requirements of Section 7609. Moreover, although these requirements are jurisdictional and their absence may be raised at any time (even on appeal), they should be raised as soon as possible.

The first requirement is found in Section 7609(b)(2)(A), which provides that the petition to quash must be filed not later than the 20th day after the noticee has been given notice. *Ponsford*, 771 F.2d 1305; *Berman*, 264 F.3d 16.[7] If that 20th day falls on a weekend or legal holiday, the last day to file the petition is the next business day. I.R.C. § 7503.

Second, Section 7609(b)(2)(B) requires the noticee who petitions to quash the summons to send by registered or certified mail copies of the petition to the summoned person and to the office designated by the Secretary of the Treasury (which is generally, but not always, the issuing IRS agent). Section 7609(b)(2)(B)'s 20-day service period for petitions to quash reflects Congress's intent to expedite summons actions and eliminate frivolous delay so that the actual investigation can proceed.

The requirements of Fed. R. Civ. P. 4(i) for service upon the United States and its agencies, corporations, officers, and employees also apply, which means that copies should be sent by registered or certified mail or delivered to the United States Attorney for the district, as well as sent by registered or certified mail to the Attorney General in Washington, D.C. *United States v. Roebuck*, 81 A.F.T.R.2d (RIA) 598, 601 (S.D. Iowa 1997) ("Rule 4's service requirements apply to petitioners proceeding under Section 7609."). *Accord Faber v. United States*, 69 F. Supp. 2d 965, 967 (W.D. Mich. 1999); *Malone v. United States*, 77 A.F.T.R.2d (RIA) 1157 (M.D. Ga. 1996); *Hartman v. United States*, 76 A.F.T.R.2d (RIA) 7856 (M.D. Fla. 1995). If a petition to quash an IRS summons is not served on the Attorney General and the United States Attorney pursuant to Rule 4(i), it is subject to dismissal. *Van Manen v. United States*, 838 F. Supp. 335, 337 (W.D. Mich. 1993) (citing former Rule 4(d)(4)), *aff'd on other grounds by unpublished opinion*, 23 F.3d 409 (6th Cir. 1994).

---

[7] One California court (in an unpublished ruling) held that the 20-day period can be subject to equitable tolling. *Mackenzie v. United States*, 84 A.F.T.R.2d (RIA) 6725, 6726-27 (E.D. Cal. 1999). In so doing, it relied on *Irwin v. Dep't of Veterans Affairs*, 498 U.S. 89 (1990). Subsequently, the Supreme Court considered whether the statute of limitation for refunds suits could be equitably tolled in light of *Irwin*, and held that equitable tolling did not apply. *United States v. Brockamp*, 519 U.S. 347 (1997). An analogous argument can be made with respect to the 20-day filing requirement to quash a summons.

The United States must be served within the 20 days mandated for mailing a copy of the petition to the IRS. *Wahler v. IRS*, 91 A.F.T.R.2d (RIA) 1731 (W.D.N.C. 2002) (service on United States must be effected within 20 days), *aff'd by unpublished opinion*, 62 Fed. Appx. 526 (4th Cir. 2003); *Norfleet v. United States*, 89 A.F.T.R.2d (RIA) 2879 (E.D.N.C.) (same), *aff'd by unpublished opinion*, 48 Fed. Appx. 907 (4th Cir. 2002); *Strong v. United States*, 57 F. Supp. 2d 908, 916 (N.D. Cal. 1999) (same); *but see Tilley v. United States*, 94 A.F.T.R.2d (RIA) 6942 (M.D.N.C. 2004) (in dictum, magistrate judge indicates 120-day period of Rule 4(m) applies); *Hicks v. United States*, 91 A.F.T.R.2d (RIA) 589 (M.D.N.C. 2003) (allowing service within 120 days); *Roebuck v. United States*, 81 A.F.T.R.2d (RIA) 598 (S.D. Iowa 1997) (same); *Hovind v. United States*, 78 A.F.T.R.2d (RIA) 7663 (dismissal for failure to serve in 120 days), *aff'd by unpublished opinion*, 159 F.3d 1359 (1998); *Tulsty v. United States*, 871 F. Supp. 299, 300 (E.D. Mich. 1994) (same).

Third, pursuant to Section 7609(h), a petition to quash must be filed in the district where the summoned party "resides or is found." This provision is a jurisdictional requirement rather than a matter of venue. *Deal v. United States*, 759 F.2d 442, 444 (5th Cir. 1985). The statute does not define "resides or is found" and the meaning of the term has been interpreted infrequently by the courts. The Ninth Circuit held that the Nevada district court did not have jurisdiction to hear a petition to quash a summons issued to a California bank. *Fortney v. United States*, 59 F.3d 117, 119 (9th Cir. 1995). The Fifth Circuit stated that jurisdiction is "vested in the district where the summons is to be answered" rather than "by the location of the taxpayer." *Masat v. United States*, 745 F.2d 985, 988 (5th Cir. 1984). *See also Beck v. United States*, 91 A.F.T.R.2d (RIA) 1345 (6th Cir. 2003). The district court in Oregon found that the statute requires "something more than the Due Process analysis of minimum contacts" and requires "a physical presence within the forum." *Oldham v. United States*, 89 A.F.T.R.2d (RIA) 2095, 2097 (D. Or. 2002). Similarly, a district court in California dismissed a petition to quash a summons issued to MasterCard International because it did not have an office in California. *Scharringhausen v. United States*, 91 A.F.T.R.2d (RIA) 651 (S.D. Cal. 2003).

b. Counterclaim for enforcement

Section 7609(b)(2)(A) permits the Government to file a counterclaim for enforcement whenever a petition to quash a summons has been filed. Whether to do so is a strategic decision to be made in consultation with the IRS. The summoned party may comply with the summons after the petition to quash the summons is dismissed or denied, without a corresponding order enforcing the summons. In such cases, a counterclaim for enforcement is unnecessary. If, on the other hand, there is a possibility that compliance would not follow, an enforcement order would be binding on the summoned party, whether or not a named party in the case. I.R.C. § 7609(b)(2)(C) ("the person summoned shall have the right to intervene. . . [and] shall be bound by the decision in such proceeding (whether or not the person intervenes in such proceeding)").

C. RESPONSES TO FREQUENT OBJECTIONS AND ARGUMENTS

In addition to claiming that the Government failed to establish the four *Powell* requirements, a summoned party or noticee may attempt a broader attack on a summons's validity. In *United States v. Powell*, 379 U.S. 48, 58 (1964), the Court explained that in a summons enforcement proceeding:

> It is the court's process which is invoked to enforce the administrative summons and a court may not permit its process to be abused. Such an abuse would take place if the summons had been issued for an improper purpose, such as to harass the taxpayer or to put pressure on him to settle a collateral dispute, or for any other purpose reflecting on the good faith of the particular investigation.

The taxpayer may "challenge the summons on any *appropriate* ground." *United States v. Freedom Church*, 613 F.2d 316, 319 (1st Cir. 1979) (citations omitted & emphasis added). The court is faced with the task of balancing the interests of the taxpayer and the Government. "On one hand is the Government's interest in summary proceedings designed to expedite tax collection. On the other hand is the taxpayer's right to protection from the *improper* use of the Internal Revenue Service's summons powers." *United States v. Stuckey*, 646 F.2d 1369, 1373 (9th Cir. 1981) (emphasis added).

In addition to broadside attacks challenging the propriety of the summons, what follows are responses to typical arguments challenging the validity of a summons.

1. IRS failed to follow administrative requirements

Taxpayers often argue that a court should not enforce a summons, or should quash a summons to a third party, because the IRS failed to follow appropriate procedures, including failure to properly issue, serve, or give notice of the summons.   In effect, such taxpayers are arguing that the fourth requirement of the *Powell* requirements has not been met. (*See* Section II(B)(2)(a)(4).)

Even if all the administrative steps required by the Code were not followed, a court may order enforcement of the summonses. Several courts have held that not every failure to follow an administrative requirement imposed by the Code necessitates denial of enforcement. *See Mimick v. United States*, 952 F.2d 230, 231-32 (8th Cir. 1991). In the words of the Fifth Circuit:

> Nothing in the language of the code itself mandates this sanction [denial of enforcement] for infringement [of the Code's administrative requirements]. The correct approach for determining whether to enforce a summons requires the court to evaluate the seriousness of the violation under all the circumstances including the Government's good faith and the degree of harm imposed by the unlawful conduct.

United States v. Payne, 648 F.2d 361, 363 (5th Cir. 1981), (quoting *United States v. Bank of Moulton*, 614 F.2d 1063, 1066 (5th Cir. 1980)).

a.   Challenges to the issuance of the summons

One of the most common challenges to summons enforcement is to the official's authority to issue the summons. Section 7602(a) provides summons authority to the "Secretary," meaning "the Secretary of the Treasury or his delegate." I.R.C. § 7701(a)(11)(B). "Delegate," in turn, is defined as "any officer, employee, or agency of the Treasury Department duly authorized by the Secretary of the Treasury directly, or indirectly by one or more redelegations of authority, to perform the function mentioned or described in the context." I.R.C. § 7701(a)(12)(A)(i).

The Secretary of the Treasury has delegated authority to issue summonses to the Commissioner of the IRS. Treas. Reg. § 301.7602-1(b) (authorizing the Commissioner of the IRS to issue summonses under I.R.C. § 7602); Treas. Reg. §301.7701-9(b) (Treasury regulations authorizing the Commissioner to perform some function "shall constitute a delegation by the Secretary of the authority to perform such function"). The Secretary has authorized the Commissioner to redelegate this authority to IRS employees. Treas. Reg. § 301.7701-9(c). The Commissioner has redelegated this authority. Deleg. Order No. 4 (Rev. 22), 1997 WL 33479254 (delegating from

Commissioner to various IRS employees, including revenue agents, authority to issue summonses).

The Supreme Court and the courts of appeal have recognized that the Secretary's authority to issue summonses has been delegated to the IRS and its employees. *See, e.g., United States v. Arthur Young & Co.*, 465 U.S. 805, 814 (1984) ("[a]s a tool of discovery, the § 7602 summons is critical to the investigative and enforcement functions of the IRS"); *United States v. Ins. Consultants of Knox, Inc.*, 187 F.3d 755, 759 (7th Cir. 1999) ("[t]he IRS is authorized to issue summonses" pursuant to I.R.C. § 7602); *Holifield v. United States*, 909 F.2d 201, 205 (7th Cir. 1990) ("The information-gathering authority granted to the IRS under § 7602 is quite broad."). Challenges to this delegation have been dismissed as lacking merit. *United States v. Derr*, 968 F.2d 943, 947 (9th Cir. 1992) (rejecting argument that IRS agents did not have delegated authority to issue summonses); *United States v. Saunders*, 951 F.2d 1065, 1067 (9th Cir. 1991) (same for summons issued by IRS Revenue Officer); *Lonsdale v. United States*, 919 F.2d 1440, 1445, 1448 (10th Cir. 1990) (failure to publish Treasury Department orders delegating authority did not deprive the IRS of authority to issue summons).

b. Challenges to service of the summons

Section 7603 provides that an IRS summons "shall be served . . . by an attested copy delivered in hand to the person to whom it is directed or left at his last and usual place of abode." *United States v. Bichara*, 826 F.2d 1037 (11th Cir. 1987) (proper service of a summons to a taxpayer does not require that the IRS leave the summons with some person of suitable age and discretion). Service "in hand" of an officer of a corporate taxpayer, including a managing agent, is sufficient to effect service on a foreign corporation. *United States v. Toyota Motor Co.*, 569 F. Supp. 1158 (C.D. Cal. 1983).

The same IRS agent or officer may both issue and serve a summons pursuant to Sections 7602 and 7603. *United States v. Crum*, 288 F.3d 332, 334 (7th Cir. 2002); *Derr*, 968 F.2d at 946-47; *United States v. McCoy*, 954 F.2d 1000, 1001 (5th Cir. 1992); *Bichara*, 826 F.2d at 1038; *United States v. Howard*, 360 F.2d 373, 375 (3d Cir. 1966).

Objections to defects in service of a summons to a third-party recordkeeper may only be raised by the summoned party; the taxpayer has no standing to assert objections to a summons that are personal to the third-party recordkeeper. *Wright v. United States*, 964 F. Supp. 336 (M.D. Fla.), *aff'd without opinion*, 132 F.3d 1461 (11th Cir. 1997).

c.   Challenges to the adequacy of the notice of the summons

While the procedural requirements of Section 7603 for serving the person named in the summons must be strictly observed, a failure to strictly comply with the taxpayer notice requirements of I.R.C. § 7609 does not necessarily warrant the quashing of third-party summonses. *United States v. Hamilton Fed. Sav. & Loan Ass'n*, 566 F. Supp. 755, 758 (E.D.N.Y. 1983). The sufficiency of the notice to the taxpayer must be judged by different standards since its only purpose is to apprise the notice of an event that has already occurred. *Id.*, citing R. Fink, Tax Fraud   Audit Investigations, Prosecutions, Vol. 1 § 7.05[2] at 7-53 (MB 1981).

To evaluate the seriousness of the facial defects, the court looks to all of the circumstances, including the Government's good faith and the prejudicial effect to the taxpayer. *Bank of Moulton*, 614 F.2d at 1066 (failure to list addresses of third parties is not prejudicial); *Tarplay v. United States*, 86 A.F.T.R.2d (RIA) 5833 (S.D.N.Y. 2000); *United States v. Hamilton Fed. Sav. & Loan Ass'n*, 566 F.Supp. at 758 (failure of the summons to properly list address of taxpayer on summons not prejudicial); *Int'l Bus. Enters. v. United States*, 75 A.F.T.R.2d (RIA) 2237 (S.D. Cal. 1995) (third-party summons will be enforced if agent makes good-faith effort to deliver a copy to taxpayer's last-known address, even though agent used the wrong address, if taxpayer actually receives notice).

Courts have enforced summonses despite defects in the timing of the notice to taxpayers. *See Cook v. United States,* 104 F.3d 886 (6th Cir. 1997) (holding that district courts possess discretionary authority to excuse the Service's technical notice errors where the party in interest suffered no actual prejudice*); Sylvestre v. United States*, 978 F.2d 25 (1st Cir. 1992) (affirming district courts refusal to quash summonses in which taxpayer was served 21 days before the date fixed for examination of records, where taxpayer had opportunity to intervene and seek to quash the summons); *Rivera v. Chase Manhattan Bank*, 53 A.F.T.R.2d (RIA) 1364 (S.D.N.Y. 1984) (absent harm to petitioner, summonses, notices of which were given to petitioner 18 and 22 days before the date set for examination, would not be quashed); *Holifield v. United States*, 677 F. Supp. 996, 998 (E.D. Wis. 1987) (although summons required third party to produce records 11 days after service of summons, in view of the fact that (a) the IRS later extended the date for production, (b) the plaintiff was able to move to quash, and (c) the records had not yet been produced, the plaintiff had not been harmed and the summons would be enforced).

Section 7603 requires that the IRS provide an attested copy of the summons to the summoned party. The majority of courts have held that the IRS need not provide an attested copy to noticees. *Kondik v. United States*, 81 F.3d 655, 657 (6th Cir. 1996) ("we hold that § 7609 requires only that taxpayers be served with copies, not attested copies"); *Fortney v. United States*, 59 F.3d 117, 120 (9th Cir. 1995) (finding that the absence of an express attestation requirement in Section 7609 is dispositive of Congress's intent); *Codner v. United States*, 17 F.3d 1331, 1334 (10th Cir. 1994) ("Congress did not intend to require that notice copies of summonses served on taxpayers be attested."); *Darland v. United States*, 921 F. Supp. 316 (D. Md. 1996). In the Eighth Circuit, however, the court held in *Mimick*, 952 F.2d at 231-32 that attested copies must be served on both the summoned party and any noticees.

d.   Other Arguments

Taxpayers have from time to time unsuccessfully alleged other procedural defects:

- In issuing summonses, the IRS is not required to comply with procedural safeguards established by the Justice Department with respect to issuing grand jury subpoenas to attorneys. *Holifield*, 909 F.2d at 205.

- There is no statute of limitations on enforcement of a summons. Being lulled and rudely awakened is not the kind of harm that allows laches to be used to deprive a plaintiff of his rights. *United States v. Admin. Enters., Inc.*, 46 F.3d 670 (7th Cir. 1995).

- The IRS is not required to complete a substitute for return prior to the issuance of a summons. *Tarplay v. United States*, 86 A.F.T.R.2d (RIA) 5833 (S.D.N.Y. 2000).

- No OMB control number is required for a summons. *Alford v. United States*, 90 A.F.T.R.2d (RIA) 7034 (N.D. Tex. 2002).

2. The summons seeks information that the summoned party has a legal duty not to reveal

A frequently encountered defense is that the summons calls for privileged documents or testimony. Only those privileges recognized under federal law, however, will be considered. *United States v. Zolin*, 491 U.S. 554, 562 (1989).

a. Attorney-client privilege

Summonses are "subject to the traditional privileges and limitations," including attorney-client privilege. *Upjohn Co. v. United States*, 449 U.S. 383, 398 (1981). The attorney-client privilege encourages "full and frank communication between attorneys and their clients and thereby promote[s] broader public interests in the observance of law and administration of justice." *Upjohn*, 449 U.S. at 389. Protecting the privilege, however, comes at a significant cost to the truth-seeking function of the adversarial system. *Zolin*, 491 U.S. at 561-63. "However, since the privilege has the effect of withholding relevant information from the fact-finder, it applies only where necessary to achieve its purpose." *Fisher v. United States*, 425 U.S. 391, 403 (1976).

A claim of attorney-client privilege will only be upheld: (1) where legal advice of any kind is sought (2) from a professional legal adviser in his capacity as such, (3) the communications relating to that purpose, (4) made in confidence (5) by the client, (6) are at his instance permanently protected (7) from disclosure by himself or by the legal adviser, (8) except the protection be waived. *See, e.g., United States v. Evans*, 113 F.3d 1457, 1461 (7th Cir. 1997) (quoting 8 John Henry Wigmore, *Evidence in Trials at Common Law* § 2292 (McNaughton rev. 1961)). The party asserting the privilege bears the burden of establishing each of the necessary elements. *Id.* at 1461; *United States v. Powell*, 379 U.S. 48, 58 (1964).

Blanket assertions of privilege are unacceptable: *Colton v. United States*, 306 F.2d 633, 639 (2d Cir. 1962); *United States v. El Paso Co.*, 682 F.2d 530, 541 (5th Cir. 1982). Claims of privilege must be made and sustained on a question-by-question and document-by-document basis.

(1) Elements of the attorney-client privilege

(i) *"Where legal advice of any kind is sought."* It is essential that the advice in question be "legal." Business advice is not covered by the privilege. *See, e.g., Sedco Int'l, S.A. v. Cory*, 683 F.2d 1201 (8th Cir. 1982); *Teltron, Inc. v. Alexander*, 132 F.R.D. 394 (E.D. Pa. 1990); *Coleman v. Am. Broad. Cos.*, 106 F.R.D. 201, 205-06 (D.D.C. 1985). Nor is the preparation of a tax return legal advice. *See, e.g., United States v. Frederick*, 182 F.3d 496 (7th Cir. 1999).

> (ii) *"From a professional legal adviser in his capacity as such."* It is not enough that a communication be made by or to a lawyer. For the privilege to apply, the lawyer must be performing services or giving advice in his capacity as a lawyer. *Evans*, 113 F.3d at 1463. The following is a list of some occasions when the privilege has been held not to apply:

- If one consults with an attorney, not as a lawyer, but as a friend or as a business advisor, the consultation is not privileged. *In re Lindsey*, 158 F.3d 1263, 1270 (D.C. Cir. 1998); *Sedco Int'l*, 683 F.2d 1201; *Colton*, 306 F.2d at 638.

- There is no privilege if the advisor is not an attorney, unless the Section 7525 privilege, discussed below, applies. (*See* Section II(C)(2)(b).) While there is no federal accountant's privilege as such, *Couch v. United States*, 409 U.S. 322, 335 (1973), there may be circumstances in which the privilege will extend to an accountant hired by an attorney to assist in his representation of the client. *Compare United States v. Kovel*, 296 F.2d 918 (2d Cir. 1961), *with Cavallaro v. United States*, 284 F.3d 236 (1st Cir. 2002), *and United States v. Ackert*, 169 F.3d 136 (2d Cir. 1999).

- When an attorney is acting as a mere scrivener the privilege does not apply. *See Canaday v. United States*, 354 F.2d 849, 857 (8th Cir. 1966) (attorney prepares tax returns); *Pollock v. United States*, 202 F.2d 281, 286 (5th Cir. 1953) ("transaction involves a simple transfer of title to real estate and there is no consultation for legal advice").

- An attorney who acts as his client's agent for receipt or disbursement of money or property to or from third parties is not acting in a legal capacity, and records of such transactions are not privileged. *In re Grand Jury Subpoena*, 831 F.2d 225, 228 (11th Cir. 1987); *Morgan v. United States*, 380 F.2d 686, 693 (9th Cir. 1967). *See* United States v. Wells, 929 F. Supp. 423 (S.D. Ga. 1996) (enforcing summons to attorney for trust account documents concerning real estate transactions of client).

- Bank records of receipts and disbursements in lawyers' trust accounts are not privileged communications. *McClary v. Walsh*, 202 F.R.D. 286 (N.D. Ala. 2000).

(iii) *"The communications relating to that purpose."* "The privilege only protects disclosure of communications; it does not protect disclosure of the underlying facts by those who communicated with the attorney . . . ." *Upjohn*, 499 U.S. at 395-96. Thus, documents do not become cloaked with the attorney-client privilege by being passed from client to lawyer, *Fisher*, 425 U.S. at 403-04, and the information that a person furnishes an attorney for the purpose of preparing his tax return is not privileged. *United States v. Lawless*, 709 F.2d 485, 488 (7th Cir. 1983).

Matters such as the client's identity, engagement letter, retainer agreement, or fees are generally not privileged. *See, e.g., United States v. BDO Seidman*, 337 F.3d 802, 811 (7th Cir. 2003) (client identity); *United States v. Leventhal*, 961 F.2d 936 (11th Cir. 1992) (fees); *United States v. Blackman*, 72 F.3d 1418 (9th Cir. 1995); *United States v. Abrahams*, 905 F.2d 1276, 1283 (9th Cir. 1990) (names of tax preparer attorney's clients and his fees were not confidential communications protected by the attorney-client privilege with respect to IRS summons); *Lefcourt v. United States*, 125 F.3d 79 (2d Cir. 1997*); United States v. Ritchie*, 15 F.3d 592 (6th Cir. 1994) (same); *Chaudhry v. Gallerizzo*, 174 F.3d 394, 402 (4th Cir. 1999); *Clarke v. Am. Commerce Nat'l Bank*, 974 F.2d 127, 129 (9th Cir. 1992); *but see United States v. Liebman* 742 F.2d 807 (3d Cir. 1984) (holding IRS could not summons names of clients lawyer had advised could take certain deductions).

Billing records which reveal the substance of confidential discussions between attorney and client, may be privileged. *In re Walsh*, 623 F.2d 489, 494-95 (7th Cir. 1980). The attorney-client privilege applies to correspondence between attorney and client which reveals the client's motivation for creation of the relationship, as well as bills, ledgers, time records and other documents which reveal the nature of the services provided. *In re Grand Jury Witness*, 695 F.2d 359, 362 (9th Cir. 1982).

To the general rule that a client's identity and the nature of his fee arrangement with his attorney are not privileged, some courts have recognized a limited exception "where disclosure would . . . constitute the 'last link' in an existing chain of evidence likely to lead to the client's indictment." *Blackman*, 72 F.3d at 1424; *see also In re Grand Jury Proceedings*, 517 F.2d 666 (5th Cir.

1975). But the last link doctrine has not met with universal acceptance, *see, e.g., Ritchie*, 15 F.3d at 602, n.13 ("our circuit has expressly rejected the last link doctrine"), and, even in circuits that have adopted it, it will not necessarily apply to prevent enforcement of an IRS summons, *see Leventhal*, 961 F.2d at 940-41.

(iv) *"Made in confidence."* There must be an expectation of confidentiality for the communication to be privileged. If the matter is not intended to remain confidential but is, for example, to be disclosed on a tax return, it is not privileged. *See Colton*, 306 F.2d at 637; *In re Grand Jury Proceedings*, 727 F.2d 1352, 1356 (4th Cir. 1984) (collecting cases). Documents transmitted to an attorney with the intent that the information will be transmitted to a third party (*e.g.*, documents needed for real estate closings and business transactions) are not protected by the attorney-client privilege. *Chevron Corp. v. Pennzoil Co.*, 974 F.2d 1156, 1162 (9th Cir. 1992) (citing *Weil v. Inv./Indicators, Research & Mgmt.*, 647 F.2d 18, 24 (9th Cir. 1981); *Lawless*, 709 F.2d at 487.

(v) *"By the client."* In order to be privileged, communications must be made by the client. Communications made by someone other than the client, even if made for the benefit of the client and even if very helpful to the attorney in rendering legal advice, are not privileged. *Ackert,* 169 F.3d at 138 ("[A] communication between an attorney and a third party does not become shielded by the attorney-client privilege solely because the communication proves important to the attorney's ability to represent the client."); *In re G-I Holdings Inc.*, 218 F.R.D. 428, 436 (D.N.J. 2003) (same). When the client is not an individual but a legal entity, such as a corporation, a court must determine which individual's communications with corporate counsel will be protected. This determination is made case by case, with an eye to identifying those persons who (1) need to obtain legal advice to perform their job and guide the corporate decision-making, and (2) are likely to have factual knowledge which the lawyer needs to know to give the best legal advice. *Upjohn,* 449 U.S. at 391-96.

(vi) *"Are at his instance permanently protected." See Swidler & Berlin v. United States*, 524 U.S. 399 (1998) (holding that the attorney-client privilege survives the death of a client, unless some other exception to the privilege applies).

(vii) *"From disclosure by himself or by the legal adviser."* An attorney need not produce documents that his client could not be compelled to produce. *Fisher,* 425 U.S. at 403-05. ("Since each taxpayer transferred possession of the documents in question from himself to his attorney in order to obtain legal assistance in the tax investigations in question, the papers, if unobtainable by summons from the client, are unobtainable by summons directed to the attorney by reason of the attorney-client privilege.").

(viii) *"Except the protection be waived."* In general, only the client can waive the attorney-client privilege, as the privilege "belongs solely to the client." *In re von Bulow,* 828 F.2d 94, 100-01 (2d Cir. 1987). An exception exists in some states which allows the personal representative of a decedent to waive the privilege in certain circumstances. *Swidler & Berlin,* 524 U.S. at 404 n.2. In the case of a corporate client, officers and directors control the privilege, which can be raised or waived. That authority, even with respect to past communications, passes to a trustee in bankruptcy who can choose to waive the privilege in light of his fiduciary duties to creditors and shareholders. *CFTC v. Weintraub,* 471 U.S. 343, 358 (1985).

(2) Express Waiver

Generally, disclosure of confidential communications or attorney work product to a third party constitutes a waiver of privilege as to those items. *See Genentech, Inc. v. United States Int'l Trade Comm'n,* 122 F.3d 1409, 1414 (Fed. Cir. 1997); *Carter v. Gibbs,* 909 F.2d 1450, 1451 (Fed. Cir. 1990) (en banc); *Clady v. County of Los Angeles,* 770 F.2d 1421, 1433 (9th Cir. 1985); *United States v. MIT* 129 F.3d 681 (1st Cir. 1997). Once the attorney-client privilege has been waived, the privilege is generally lost for all purposes and in all forums. *Genentech,* 122 F.3d at 1416. Voluntary disclosure of a privileged document waives the attorney-client privilege with respect to all communications on the same subject matter. *Weil,* 647 F.2d at 24; *Golden Valley Microwave Foods, Inc. v. Weaver Popcorn Co.,* 132 F.R.D. 204, 207-08 (N.D. Ind. 1990); *Standard Chartered Bank, PLC v. Ayala Int'l Holding, Inc.,* 111 F.R.D. 76, 85 (S.D.N.Y. 1986).

(3) Implied Waiver

A party may waive the attorney-client privilege by asserting claims or defenses that put his or her attorney's advice at issue in the litigation. *Rhone-Poulenc Rorer, Inc. v. Home Indem. Co.,* 32 F.3d 851, 863 (3d Cir. 1994). *See Chevron,* 974 F.2d 1156 (party's claim that its tax position was reasonable because it was based on advice of counsel puts advice at issue and waives privilege). Common factors in finding implied waiver are (1) assertion of the privilege is a result of an affirmative act; (2) through the affirmative act, the asserting party has placed the protected information at issue by making it relevant; and (3) application of privilege would deny the opposing party access to information vital to its defense. *Hearn v. Rhay*, 68 F.R.D. 574 (E.D. Wash. 1975).

The doctrine of waiver by implication reflects the position that the attorney-client privilege may not be used as both a sword and a shield. *Chevron*, 974 F.2d at 1162; *In re Bilzerian*, 926 F.2d 1285, 1292 (2d Cir. 1991); *In re von Bulow*, 828 F.2d at 103. In other words, "[a] defendant may not use the privilege to prejudice his opponent's case or to disclose some selected communications for self-serving purposes." *Bilzerian,* 926 F.2d at 1292; *accord United States v. Jones,* 696 F.2d 1069, 1072 (4th Cir. 1982) ("Selective disclosure for tactical purposes waives the privilege.").

Where a waiver has been found, the courts have taken at least three different approaches in defining the scope of the waiver:

- The scope of the waiver only extends to the specific documents produced: *Prudential Ins. Co. v. Turner & Newall, PLC*, 137 F.R.D. 178, 182 (D. Mass. 1991); *Parkway Gallery Furniture, Inc. v. Kittinger/Pa. House Group, Inc.*, 116 F.R.D. 46, 52 (M.D.N.C. 1987); *Int'l Digital Sys. Corp. v. Digital Equip. Corp.*, 120 F.R.D. 445, 446 (D. Mass. 1988).

- The scope of the waiver encompasses all privileged materials *on the same* subject matter as the produced documents: *Standard Chartered Bank*, 111 F.R.D. at 85; *Perrignon v. Bergen Brunswig Corp.*, 77 F.R.D. 455, 461 (N.D. Cal. 1978); *Goldman, Sachs & Co. v. Blondis*, 412 F. Supp. 286, 289 (N.D. Ill. 1976).

- The scope of the waiver includes all privileged documents *relating to* the same subject matter as the produced documents: *In re Sealed Case*, 877 F.2d 976, 977 (D.C. Cir. 1989).

(4) Selective Waiver

In *Diversified Indus., Inc. v. Meredith*, 572 F.2d 596 (8th Cir. 1977) (en banc), the Eighth Circuit held that the corporate defendant had *not* waived the attorney-client privilege when it disclosed to the SEC certain memoranda and other documents prepared by special outside counsel who had been retained to investigate certain practices of the company's personnel. The court of appeals concluded that only a "limited" waiver had occurred, thereby giving rise to what has come to be called the "selective" waiver doctrine. As its only reason for its conclusion, the court stated that "[t]o hold otherwise may have the effect of thwarting the developing procedure of corporations to employ independent outside counsel to investigate and advise them in order to protect stockholders, potential stockholders and customers." *Id.* at 611.

The doctrine has not achieved much traction, as most courts have refused to apply it. *See, e.g.*, *In re Columbia/HCA Healthcare Corp.*, 293 F.3d 289, 302 (6th Cir. 2002) ("we reject the concept of selective waiver, in any of its various forms"); *MIT*, 129 F.3d 681 (disclosure normally negates the privilege); *Dellwood Farms, Inc. v. Cargill, Inc.*, 128 F.3d 1122, 1126 (7th Cir. 1997) ("The cases . . . generally reject a right of 'selective' waiver, where, having voluntarily disclosed privileged information to one person, the party who made the disclosure asserts the privilege against another person who wants the information."); *Genentech*, 122 F.3d 1409 (rejecting selective waiver doctrine to allegedly inadvertent disclosure); *In re Steinhardt Partners, LP*, 9 F.3d 230 (2d Cir. 1993) (refusing to apply selective waiver doctrine to voluntary disclosure of work product to SEC); *Westinghouse Elec. Corp. v. Republic of the Philippines*, 951 F.2d 1414 (3d Cir. 1991) (rejecting application of selective waiver doctrine); *In re Martin Marietta Corp.*, 856 F.2d 619 (4th Cir. 1988) (same); *Permian Corp. v. United States*, 665 F.2d 1214, 1220 (D.C. Cir. 1981) (finding selective waiver theory "wholly unpersuasive"); *but see United States v. Bergonzi*, 403 F.3d 1048, 1050 (9th Cir. 2005) (per curiam) ("Whether the sort of selective waiver McKesson seeks is available in this Circuit is an open question.") (citing *Bittaker v. Woodford*, 331 F.3d 715, 720 n.5 (9th Cir. 2003) (en banc) ("[T]he law [regarding selective waiver] is not . . . settled.")).

The Tax Division's view has been that selective waiver would extend the privilege beyond its intended purpose of encouraging full disclosure to one's attorney in order to obtain informed legal assistance. In *MIT*, 129 F.3d 681, the Tax Division successfully contended that MIT had forfeited attorney-client privilege and work-product protection for documents that had been disclosed to the Defense Contract Audit Agency. MIT thus had to turn over the documents in response to an IRS summons.

(5) Inadvertent Waiver

A voluntary disclosure of information that is inconsistent with the confidential nature of the attorney-client relationship waives the privilege. *Alldread v. City of Grenada*, 988 F.2d 1425, 1434 (5th Cir. 1993). There is no consensus, however, as to the effect of inadvertent disclosure. Some courts hold that where there has been a disclosure of privileged communications to third parties, the privilege is lost, even if the disclosure is unintentional or inadvertent. *See In re Sealed Case*, 877 F.2d at 980; *In re Grand Jury Proceedings*, 727 F.2d at 1356.

The majority of courts, while recognizing that inadvertent disclosure may result in a waiver of the privilege, have incorporated an approach which takes into account the facts surrounding a particular disclosure. *Alldread*, 988 F.2d at 1434. Courts generally apply the following factors in determining whether inadvertent disclosure should be treated as a waiver of attorney-client privilege:

> the reasonableness of the precautions to prevent inadvertent disclosure, the time taken to rectify the error, the scope of the discovery and the extent of the disclosure. There is, of course, an overreaching issue of fairness and the protection of an appropriate privilege which, of course, must be judged against the care or negligence with which the privilege is guarded.

Lois Sportswear, USA, Inc. v. Levi Strauss & Co. 104 F.R.D. 103, 105 (S.D.N.Y. 1985); *Dellwood Farms*, 128 F.3d at 1127.

The ABA has issued an opinion stating that a lawyer who receives materials that on their face appear to be subject to the attorney-client privilege or otherwise confidential, under circumstances where it is clear that they were not intended for the receiving lawyer, should refrain from examining the materials, notify the sending lawyer and abide the instructions of the lawyer who sent them. ABA Comm. on Ethics and Prof'l Responsibility, Formal Op. 368 (1992). An attorney who receives such materials should confer with his or her supervisor.

May 2006

(6) Crime Fraud Exception

The attorney-client privilege does not extend to communications "in furtherance of intended or present continuing illegality." *In re Grand Jury Proceedings,* 87 F.3d 377, 381 (9th Cir. 1996); *United States v. Jacobs,* 117 F.3d 82, 87 (2d Cir. 1997). When a client abuses the system by consulting an attorney for the purpose of furthering criminal or fraudulent activity, the application of the attorney-client privilege is overcome by the "crime-fraud exception" and such information loses its protected status. *Zolin,* 491 U.S. at 561-63. *See also Clark v. United States,* 289 U.S. 1 (1933). In such circumstances, the value to society of encouraging attorney-client communications is outweighed by "the costs of probative evidence foregone." *In re Grand Jury Proceedings (Violette),* 183 F.3d 71, 76 (1st Cir. 1991).

The party seeking application of the crime-fraud exception to overcome the attorney-client privilege must make the following prima facie showing:

> (1) that the client was engaged in (or was planning) criminal or fraudulent activity when the attorney-client communications took place; *and* (2) that the communications were intended by the client to facilitate or conceal the criminal or fraudulent activity.

Violette, 183 F.3d at 75 (emphasis in original). The exception applies not only where the client actually knows that the contemplated activity is illegal, but also where the client "reasonably should have known." *United States v. Rakes,* 136 F.3d 1, 4 (1st Cir. 1998). Moreover, whether the attorney knew about or was complicit in the illegal activity has no bearing on the crime-fraud determination. *See United States v. Reeder,* 170 F.3d 93, 106 (1st Cir.), *cert. denied,* 528 U.S. 872 (1999); *In re Grand Jury Investigation,* 842 F.2d 1223, 1226 (11th Cir. 1987); *Jacobs,* 117 F.3d at 87. The moving party must also establish "some relationship between the communications at issue and the alleged offense." *Sound Video Unlimited, Inc. v. Video Shack, Inc.,* 661 F. Supp. 1482, 1486 (N.D. Ill. 1987). Prima facie evidence is a "lax standard." *In re Feldberg,* 862 F.2d 622, 626 (7th Cir. 1988).

To determine whether the crime-fraud exception applies, the court may conduct an in camera review of the alleged communications. "[A] lesser evidentiary showing is needed to trigger *in camera* review than is required to ultimately overcome the privilege." *Zolin,* 491 U.S. at 572.

Once that showing is made, the decision whether to engage in *in camera* review rests in the sound discretion of the district court. The court should make that decision in light of the facts and circumstances of the particular case, including, among other things, the volume of materials the district court has been asked to review, the relative importance to the case of the alleged privileged information, and the likelihood that the evidence produced through *in camera* review, together with other available evidence then before the court, will establish that the crime-fraud exception does apply.

Id.

Whether or not there has been an in camera review, the district court exercises its discretion again to determine whether the facts are such that the crime-fraud exception applies. *Jacobs*, 117 F.3d at 87. Mere allegations or suspicion by the Government are insufficient. But proof beyond a reasonable doubt is not necessary to justify application of the crime-fraud exception. The test for invoking the crime-fraud exception to the attorney-client privilege is whether there is "reasonable cause to believe that the attorney's services were utilized in furtherance of the ongoing unlawful scheme." Reasonable cause is more than suspicion but less than a preponderance of evidence. *In re Grand Jury Proceedings,* 87 F.3d at 381 (9th Cir. 1996) (citation omitted).

The crime-fraud exception is not limited to traditional criminal activities; the crime-fraud exception has been applied to civil fraud, as well as criminal fraud. *See United States v. Ballard*, 779 F.2d 287 (5th Cir. 1986) (communications relating to a fraudulent conveyance and scheme to conceal assets from bankruptcy court are not protected by the attorney-client privilege); *United States v. Barrier Indus., Inc.*, 1997 WL 16668 (S.D.N.Y. 1997); *In re Rigby*, 199 B.R. 358 (E.D. Tex. 1995) (crime-fraud exception applies to communications in furtherance of scheme to partition property to avoid IRS lien; exception applies to work-product privilege as well).

b. Tax Practitioner privilege - § 7525

Prior to the Internal Revenue Service Restructuring and Reform Act of 1998, Pub. L. No. 105-206, 112 Stat. 685, the attorney-client privilege was limited to a communication between a client and her lawyer. And the Supreme Court had ruled in *Couch*, 409 U.S. at 335, that "no confidential accountant-client privilege exists under federal law, and no state-created

44

privilege has been recognized in federal cases." So things stood until 1998, when Congress added Section 7525 to the Code.

With respect to communications made on or after July 22, 1998, Section 7525(a)(1) provides that "[w]ith respect to tax advice, the same common law protections of confidentiality which apply to a communication between a taxpayer and an attorney shall also apply to a communication between a taxpayer and any federally authorized tax practitioner to the extent the communication would be considered a privileged communication if it were between a taxpayer and an attorney." A "federally authorized tax practitioner" is "any individual who is authorized under Federal law to practice before the Internal Revenue Service if such practice is subject to Federal regulation under section 330 of title 31, United States Code." I.R.C. § 7525(a)(3)(A). "Tax advice" is defined as "advice given by an individual with respect to a matter which is within the scope of the individual's authority to practice [before the IRS]." I.R.C. § 7525(a)(3)(B).

Section 7525 only "protects communications between a taxpayer and a federally authorized tax practitioner 'to the extent the communication would be considered a privileged communication if it were between a taxpayer and an attorney.'" *Frederick,* 182 F.3d at 502 (quoting I.R.C. § 7525(a)(1)). The scope of the Section 7525 privilege is thus no broader than that of the attorney-client privilege and is subject to all the limitations and restrictions imposed on the attorney-client privilege at common law. For example, the Conference Committee report notes that the Section 7525 privilege may be waived by disclosure to third parties in the same way as is true of the attorney-client privilege. H.R. Conf. Rep. No. 105-599, at 267 (1998), *reprinted in* 1998-3 C.B. 755, 1023.

The Section 7525 privilege is subject to special statutory limitations that otherwise make it significantly narrower than the attorney-client privilege. The privilege, such as it is, may only be asserted in any *noncriminal* tax matter before the IRS and in any *noncriminal* tax proceeding in Federal court brought by or against the United States. I.R.C. § 7525(a)(2). As a consequence, it is *not* available in response to a summons issued by an IRS special agent pursuing a criminal investigation. So, too, it is not available in any non-tax matter or proceeding, whether or not the IRS or the United States is a party. Thus, it "may not be asserted to prevent the disclosure of information to any regulatory body other than the IRS." S. Rep. No. 105-174, at 71 (1998), *reprinted in* 1998-3 C.B. 537, 607.

With respect to communications made before October 22, 2004, Section 7525(b) provides that the privilege "shall *not* apply to any written communication which is between a federally authorized tax practitioner and any director, officer, employee, agent, or representative of the person, or any other person holding a capital or profits interest in the person, and in connection with the promotion of the direct or indirect participation of the person in any tax shelter." (Emphasis added.) For these purposes, Section 7525(b) incorporates Section 6662(d)(2)(C)(ii)'s broad definition of the term "tax shelter" as "(I) a partnership or other entity, (II) any investment plan or arrangement, or (III) any other plan or arrangement, if a significant purpose of such partnership, entity, plan, or arrangement is the avoidance or evasion of Federal income tax."

With respect to communications made on or after October 22, 2004, Section 7525(b) was amended by the American Jobs Creation Act of 2004, Pub. L. No. 108-357, § 813, 118 Stat.1418, 1581, to make the tax practitioner privilege inapplicable to any written communication in connection with the promotion of the direct or indirect participation of any person in such a tax shelter, whether or not the participant is a corporation.

Among the cases to consider contentions that the Section 7525 privilege applied are:

- *BDO Seidman*, 337 F.3d 802 (applying attorney-client privilege law to reject claim that a client's identity was a matter of privilege under Section 7525);

- *Scotty's Contracting & Stone, Inc. v. United States*, 326 F.3d 785 (6th Cir. 2003) (rejecting suggestion that *Arthur Young* is no longer good law in light of Section 7525);

- *Doe v. KPMG, LLP*, 325 F. Supp. 2d 746 (N.D. Tex. 2004) (rejecting claim that client identities were privileged under Section 7525), *rev'd on other grounds*, 398 F.3d 686 (5th Cir. 2005);

- *Doe v. Wachovia Corp.*, 268 F. Supp. 2d 627 (W.D.N.C. 2003) (finding Section 7525 inapplicable where the United States was not a party, there was no IRS tax proceeding, and the tax shelter involved a corporation);

- *United States v. KPMG, LLP*, 237 F. Supp. 2d 35 (D.D.C. 2002) (finding Section 7525 did not apply to communications relating to preparation of tax returns).

c. Work product

In general, the work-product doctrine, now embodied in Fed. R. Civ. P. 26(b)(3), provides qualified protection for documents:

> prepared in anticipation of litigation or for trial by or for another party or by or for that other party's representative (including the other party's attorney, consultant, surety, indemnitor, insurer, or agent) only upon a showing that the party seeking discovery has substantial need of the materials in the preparation of the party's case and that the party is unable without undue hardship to obtain the substantial equivalent of the materials by other means. In ordering discovery of such materials when the required showing has been made, the court shall protect against disclosure of the mental impressions, conclusions, opinions, or legal theories of an attorney or other representative of a party concerning the litigation.

The question whether a document was prepared in anticipation of litigation is often a difficult factual matter. *United States v. Rockwell Int'l,* 897 F. 2d 1255 (3d Cir. 1990). In *United States v. Adlman,* 134 F. 3d 1194 (2d Cir. 1998), the Court of Appeals held that a memorandum prepared by outside accountants analyzing likely IRS challenges to a corporate reorganization was protected work-product. The court accepted, without question, the taxpayer's assertion that litigation "was virtually certain to result" from the proposed transaction if carried out, because the IRS usually audited the taxpayer's returns, the claimed refund was so large it would require approval from the Joint Congressional Committee on Taxation under section 6405, and there was no case or IRS ruling exactly on point which would validate the transaction. *Id.* at 1196. The court held that "a document created because of anticipated litigation, which tends to reveal mental impressions, conclusions, opinions or theories concerning the litigation, does not lose work-product protection merely because it is intended to assist in the making of a business decision influenced by the likely outcome of the anticipated litigation. *Id.* at 1195. In the course of its opinion, the Second Circuit rejected what it viewed as a narrower standard, described as "principal purpose" or "primarily to assist in" litigation, as opposed to primarily to assist in making a business decision. *See also, In re Grand Jury Subpoena*, 357 F.3d 900, 908 (9th Cir. 2004). In any event, anticipation of an IRS audit does not amount to anticipation of litigation and a factual record can be made to establish this point.

In *United States v. Baggot*, 463 U.S. 476, 484 (1983), the Supreme Court held that an IRS civil audit was not "preliminarily to or in connection with a judicial proceeding" within the meaning of Fed. R. Crim. P. 6(e)(3)(C)(I). As a result, grand jury transcripts and documents could not be disclosed for use in the audit. Although the Court noted, 463 U.S. at 479 n.3, that its decision was limited to Rule 6(e)(3)(C)(I) and that "[o]ther considerations may govern the construction of similar standards in other contexts (*e.g.*, Fed. R. Civ. P. 26(b)(3) ('in anticipation of litigation or for trial'))," its opinion is nonetheless instructive.

The Court explained the "preliminarily to" requirement as follows:

[T]he Rule contemplates only uses related fairly directly to some identifiable litigation, pending or anticipated. Thus, it is not enough to show that some litigation may emerge from the matter in which the material is to be used, or even that litigation is factually likely to emerge. The focus is on the *actual use* to be made of the material. If the primary purpose of disclosure is not to assist in preparation or conduct of a judicial proceeding, disclosure under (C)(i) is not permitted.

Baggot, 463 U.S. at 480 (emphasis in original). In other words, a civil tax audit does not in and of itself portend litigation. The *Baggot* Court recognized that there are four possible outcomes of a civil audit, three of which may involve litigation at some point in the future. *Id.* Nevertheless, the Court held that an audit was not "preliminarily to" litigation:

The fact that judicial redress may be sought, without more, does not mean that the Government's action is "preliminar[y] to a judicial proceeding." Of course, it may often be loosely said that the Government's action is "preparing for litigation," in the sense that frequently it will be wise for an agency to anticipate the chance that it may be called upon to defend its actions in court. That, however, is not alone enough to bring an administrative action within (C)(i). Where an agency's action does not require resort to litigation to

accomplish the agency's present goal, the action is not preliminary to
a judicial proceeding for purposes of (C)(i).

Id. at 481-82. *See also, Culinary Foods, Inc. v. Raychem Corp.*, 150 F.R.D.
122, 130 (N.D. Ill. 1993) (documents prepared during OSHA investigation not
in anticipation of litigation because, in OSHA cases, litigation generally is
contemplated only after the employer refuses to recognize and correct safety
violations).

While the Supreme Court, with citation to Fed. R. Civ. P. 26(b)(3), has
held that the work-product doctrine protects "material prepared by agents for
the attorney as well as those prepared by the attorney himself" (*United States
v. Nobles*, 422 U.S. 225, 238-39 (1975)), and applies to summons enforcement
proceedings, *Upjohn*, 449 U.S. at 398-99, the Court also has held that there is
no work-product immunity for the tax accrual work papers prepared by an
accountant on behalf of a corporation. *See United States v. Arthur Young &
Co.*, 465 U.S. 805, 817 (1984). *(See*, Section II.B.2.c.(3).) Work-product
protection turns, in substantial part, on the role of the person preparing the
sought-after document. When an accountant is in the role of auditor of a
public company, his memoranda are not created "because of" litigation. An
outside auditor is performing a very different function than a business or tax
advisor. It is important in each case to set forth a factual record
demonstrating the work done and the role of the document creator.

Privilege for work-product, other than the mental impressions of an
attorney, may be overcome with a showing of substantial need. In the
summons enforcement context, a factual record needs to be made to establish
the substantial need for non-opinion work-product. Attorney opinion work-
product, on the other hand, receives special protection by the courts; it is not
available even upon a showing of substantial need. *See Pacamor Bearings,
Inc. v. Minebea Co.*, 918 F. Supp. 491 (D.N.H. 1996) (attorney opinion work-
product distinguished from "ordinary" work-product); *Fraiser v. Southeastern
Pa. Transp. Auth.*, 161 F.R.D. 309 (E.D. Pa. 1995) (same).

Finally, it must be recalled that while I.R.C. § 7525 creates a tax
practitioner privilege analogous to the attorney-client communication
privilege, it does *not* create a work-product privilege apart from that created
by Rule 26(b)(3). *Frederick*, 182 F.3d at 502.

3. Overly broad, vague, or burdensome

As an adjunct to arguments attacking the relevance of summoned materials, parties resisting enforcement of IRS summonses frequently assert that summonses are so broad, indefinite, or burdensome as to constitute an unreasonable search in violation of the Fourth Amendment. To pass constitutional muster, however, all that is required is that the summons describe the documents with sufficient particularity and not be excessive for the purposes of the inquiry. *See Oklahoma Press Pub'g Co. v. Walling*, 327 U.S. 186, 209 (1946). "As for specificity, the summons [need only describe] the requested documents in enough detail to inform [the summoned party] of exactly what he was to produce." *United States v. Abrahams*, 905 F.2d 1276, 1282 (9th Cir. 1990). *See also United States v. Judicial Watch, Inc.*, 371 F.3d 824, 832 (D.C. Cir. 2004)*; United States v. Medlin*, 986 F.2d 463, 467 (11th Cir. 1993) ("An IRS summons is overbroad if it 'does not advise the summoned party what is required of him with sufficient specificity to permit him to respond adequately to the summons.'" (quoting *United States v. Wyatt,* 637 F.2d 293, 302 n.16 (5th Cir. 1981))).

While the Commissioner's summons authority has been described as a license to fish, *United States v. Luther*, 481 F.2d 429, 432-33 (9th Cir. 1973) ("Sec. 7602 authorizes the Secretary or his delegate 'to fish'"); *United States v. Giordano*, 419 F.2d 564, 568 (8th Cir. 1969) ("Secretary or his delegate has been specifically licensed to fish by § 7602"), this license is not without limit. The IRS may not conduct an unfettered "fishing expedition" through a person's records, but "must identify with some precision the documents it wishes to inspect." *United States v. Dauphin Deposit Trust Co.*, 385 F.2d 129, 131 (3d Cir. 1967). Thus, in testing for overbreadth, the question is not whether the summons calls for the production of a large volume of records. Instead, the questions are rather, first did the summons describe the requested documents in enough detail to inform the summoned party of exactly what is to be produced, *Abrahams*, 905 F.2d at 1282, 1285, and, second, may the summoned records be relevant to the inquiry. *In re Tax Liabs. of John Does v. United States*, 866 F.2d 1015, 1021 (8th Cir. 1989). Summonses that are definite in nature and finite in scope, and that request only information that may be relevant to the IRS's inquiry, consistently have been enforced against challenges for overbreadth. *See, e.g., United States v. Reis,* 765 F.2d 1094, 1096 n.2 (11th Cir. 1985); *United States v. Linsteadt*, 724 F.2d 480, 483 n.1 (5th Cir. 1984); *United States v. Cmty. Fed. Sav. & Loan*

Ass'n, 661 F.2d 694 (8th Cir. 1981); *United States v. Nat'l Bank of South Dakota*, 622 F.2d 365 (8th Cir. 1980).

Likewise, the courts have not been receptive to arguments that a summons may be overly burdensome to the summoned party. It is now well established that enforcement of a summons seeking relevant records will not be denied merely because the summons seeks production of (or a search through) a great many records or will result in significant expenditure of the recordkeeper's time and money. *See, e.g., Judicial Watch*, 371 F.3d at 832; *Spell v. United States*, 907 F.2d 36, 39 (4th Cir. 1990); *United States v. Berney*, 713 F.2d 568, 571-72 (10th Cir. 1983); *Luther*, 481 F.2d at 432-33; *In re Tax Liabs. of John Does*, 866 F.2d at 1021 (court rejected employer's claim that the cost of compliance with summons seeking payroll records for 50 employees was out of proportion to any revenue that the IRS might obtain); *United States v. Southwestern Bank & Trust Co.*, 693 F.2d 994, 996 (10th Cir. 1982) (reversing district court's refusal to enforce fully a summons requiring review of 10 million documents).

4. First Amendment privilege

The First Amendment to the United States Constitution prohibits the Government from "abridging the freedom of speech." The Government may investigate speech, either spoken or written, only if it is outside the First Amendment's protection.

Courts may quash IRS administrative summonses that would infringe on First Amendment rights   either those of the speaker or those of the speaker's audience. *United States v. Trader's State Bank*, 695 F.2d 1132 (9th Cir. 1983) (per curiam) (vacating an order of enforcement of an IRS summons seeking all church banking records as overbroad and an infringement on the church's First Amendment rights of freedom of association and freedom of religion); *United States v. Citizens State Bank*, 612 F.2d 1091, 1094 (8th Cir. 1980) (holding that the district court erred in failing to consider First Amendment implications of IRS summons). The right to speak or write anonymously is an inherent part of First Amendment freedoms, as are the rights to participate in an organization, listen to a speaker, or read anonymously. *See generally McIntyre v. Ohio Elections Comm'n*, 514 U.S. 334 (1995).

If the summoned party can make a "prima facie showing of arguable first amendment infringement," then, before a court will enforce the summons, the

Government must demonstrate "a rational connection between the disclosure required by the summons and a legitimate governmental end, and must demonstrate a cogent and compelling governmental interest in the disclosure." *Trader's State Bank*, 695 F.2d at 1133. The effect of this standard is that the IRS summons should be narrowly drafted to avoid First Amendment implications.

It is not illegal merely to advocate a false tax theory. *See generally Virginia v. Black*, 538 U.S. 343, 358 (2003) ("the First Amendment 'ordinarily' denies a State 'the power to prohibit dissemination of social, economic and political doctrine which a vast majority of its citizens believes to be false and fraught with evil consequence.'") (quoting *Whitney v. California*, 274 U.S. 357, 374 (1927)); *Texas v. Johnson*, 491 U.S. 397, 414 (1989) ("If there is a bedrock principle underlying the First Amendment, it is that the government may not prohibit the expression of an idea simply because society finds the idea itself offensive or disagreeable.").

Unless the speech falls into one of three unprotected or less-protected categories, a court will not permit the Government to restrict or otherwise interfere with speech. The three categories, which often overlap, are: (a) false commercial speech, (b) speech that is part of a course of illegal conduct, and (c) speech that incites others to imminently violate the law. *Ohralik v. Ohio State Bar Ass'n*, 436 U.S. 447, 455-56 (1978); *Brandenburg v. Ohio*, 395 U.S. 444, 448-49 (1969).

(a) The First Amendment does not protect false commercial speech. Commercial speech is entitled to less protection under the First Amendment than political speech, and so can more easily be regulated or enjoined. *Virginia State Bd. of Pharmacy v. Virginia Citizens Consumer Council, Inc.*, 425 U.S. 748, 771-72 (1976) (holding that commercial speech is protected by the First Amendment, but that the Government may regulate false commercial speech). The Supreme Court has held that the Government "may ban commercial expression that is fraudulent or deceptive without further justification." *Edenfield v. Fane*, 507 U.S. 761, 768 (1993). Commercial speech, however, is subject to injunction *only* if it is false or misleading; otherwise, it is protected by the First Amendment. *See, e.g., United States v. Estate Pres. Servs.*, 202 F.3d 1093, 1096 n.3, 1097, 1099, 1106 (9th Cir. 2000) (enjoining as "fraudulent conduct" and misleading "commercial speech" the "marketing" and "selling" of a "training manual" that provided "false tax advice"); *United States v. Raymond*, 228 F.3d 804, 807, 815 (7th Cir. 2000) (enjoining as "false or misleading commercial speech" advertisements and a three-volume book); *United States v. Schiff*, 379 F.3d 621 (9th Cir. 2004) (affirming ban on sale of the book titled FEDERAL MAFIA, containing autobiographical information and Schiff's anti-tax theories, but also offering instructions on how to fraudulently complete an IRS W-4 Form and providing a two-page attachment for customers to submit to the IRS with their "zero-income" Forms 1040), *petition for cert. filed*, 73 U.S.L.W. 3632 (U.S. Apr. 12, 2005) (No. 04-13); *NCBA/NCE v. United States*, 843 F. Supp. 655, 665 (D. Colo. 1993) ("Perhaps the NCBA Freedom Books, standing alone, would amount to mere advocacy. But the NCBA went so far as to establish the NCE [a warehouse bank] and tout the privacy it afforded to members. The NCE was clearly established to thwart enforcement of the tax laws, and as such was an abusive tax shelter."), *aff'd by unpublished opinion,* 42 F.3d 1406 (10th Cir. 1994) .

(b) The First Amendment does not protect speech that is itself part of a course of illegal conduct. Speech directed toward committing a crime for example, conspiracy or tax fraud can itself be "conduct." Banning a course of conduct does not violate the First Amendment "'merely because the conduct was in part initiated, evidenced, or carried out by means of language, either spoken, written, or printed.'" *Ohralik*, 436 U.S. at 456 (citation omitted). *See Vill. of Hoffman Estates v. Flipside, Hoffman Estates, Inc.*, 455 U.S. 489, 496 (1982) (holding that "the government may regulate or ban entirely" "speech proposing an illegal transaction"). The Supreme Court has emphasized that the First Amendment "does not shield fraud," *Madigan v. Telemarketing Assocs., Inc.*, 538 U.S 600, 612 (2003), and has pointed to "[n]umerous examples . . . of communications that are regulated without offending the First Amendment, such as the exchange of information about securities, corporate proxy statements, the exchange of price and production information among competitors, and employers' threats of retaliation for the labor activities of employees." *Ohralik*, 436 U.S. at 456 (citations omitted); *see also Pittsburgh Press Co. v. Pittsburgh Comm'n on Human Relations*, 413 U.S. 376, 389 (1973) (order prohibiting newspaper from publishing discriminatory advertisement); *Nat'l Soc'y of Prof'l Eng'rs v. United States*, 435 U.S. 679, 696-699 (1978) (injunction against publication of ethical canon); *NLRB v. Retail Store Employees Union*, 447 U.S. 607, 616 (1980) (ban on secondary picketing).

(c) The First Amendment does not protect speech that incites others to imminently violate tax laws. The "incitement" line of cases began with *Brandenburg v. Ohio*, in which the Supreme Court, examining whether the First Amendment applied to statements to an angry mob, held that First

Amendment protection turned on whether the surrounding circumstances the context in which the statements were made made it likely that the statements would incite others to imminent lawlessness. 395 U.S. at 448-49. Since *Brandenburg*, courts have focused on the "imminence" part of this test. Injunctions prohibiting tax scheme advocacy have been upheld under *Brandenburg* where customers were persuaded and followed the promoter's advice. *See Raymond*, 228 F.3d at 815; *United States v. Kaun*, 827 F.2d 1144, 1150-52 (7th Cir. 1987). Every circuit that has addressed the issue has "concluded that the First Amendment is generally inapplicable to charges of aiding and abetting violations of the tax laws." *Rice v. Paladin Enters., Inc.*, 128 F.3d 233, 245 (4th Cir. 1997) (collecting cases).

5. Fourth Amendment privilege

Powell does not require a showing of probable cause. *United States v. Powell*, 379 U.S. 48, 51 (1964); *United States v. White*, 853 F.2d 107, 109 (2d Cir. 1988) ("[W]e find the district court's summons enforcement requirement that the IRS must make a prima facie showing of 'fraud, overreaching, or excessiveness by the attorney or the Surrogate' to be inconsistent with *Powell*'s holding that only a showing of a legitimate purpose, and not a showing of probable cause, is required for summons enforcement of its summonses and we therefore reverse."). A summons which complies with the *Powell* requirements and is narrowly drawn satisfies the Fourth Amendment. *Fisher v. United States*, 425 U.S. 391, 401 n.7 (1976). "A summons is not overbroad for the purpose of the Fourth Amendment ban on 'unreasonable searches and seizures' if the inquiry is 'within the authority of the agency, the demand is not too indefinite[,] and the information sought is reasonably relevant.'" *United States v. Judicial Watch, Inc.*, 371 F.3d 824, 833 (D.C. Cir. 2004) (citing *United States v. Morton Salt Co.*, 338 U.S. 632, 652-53 (1950) and *Oklahoma Press Publ'g Co. v. Walling*, 327 U.S. 186, 209 (1946)). *See also Cypress Funds, Inc. v. United States*, 234 F.3d 1267 (6th Cir. 2000); *United States v. Abrahams*, 905 F.2d 1276, 1282 (9th Cir. 1990); *United States v. McAnlis*, 721 F.2d 334, 337 (11th Cir. 1983); *United States v. Roundtree*, 420 F.2d 845, 849-50 (5th Cir. 1969).[8]

---

[8] In *Richard A. Vaughn, DDS, P.C. v. Baldwin*, 950 F.2d 331 (6th Cir. 1991), the court concluded that the Fourth Amendment applied to the IRS's retention of records voluntarily turned over in response to a summons once that consent was withdrawn. Once consent is withdrawn, the United States must obtain a court order. *See also, Linn v. Chivatero*, 714 F.2d 1278, 1284 (5th Cir. 1983); *Mason v.*

A taxpayer's Fourth Amendment rights are not implicated by a summons to a third party. *Donaldson v. United States*, 400 U.S. 517 (1971); *United States v. Miller*, 425 U.S. 435, 440-44 (1976) ("Since no Fourth Amendment interests of the depositor are implicated here, this case is governed by the general rule that the issuance of a subpoena to a third party to obtain the records of that party does not violate the rights of a defendant, even if a criminal prosecution is contemplated at the time of the subpoena is issued.").

A summons which is alleged to have resulted from an unconstitutional search or other Fourth Amendment violation, however, may be challenged on Fourth Amendment grounds. *United States v. Beacon Fed. Savings & Loan*, 718 F.2d 49, 54 (2d Cir. 1983) (taxpayer alleged that enforcement of summonses should be denied because they are part of an investigation that was intensified as the result of an unconstitutional search and seizure by the revenue agent). A taxpayer must make a substantial preliminary showing of a Fourth Amendment violation before a court will entertain such allegations. *Id.* A summons may be used, however, to obtain documents previously suppressed in a criminal case because of an improper search, so long as there is an independent source for knowledge of documents. *McGarry's, Inc. v. Rose*, 344 F.2d 416, 418 (1st Cir. 1965) (permitting use of an administrative summons to obtain documents previously seized in violation of the Fourth Amendment because IRS agent had knowledge of the documents independent of the unlawful seizure); *United States v. Heubusch*, 295 F. Supp. 2d 240 (W.D.N.Y. 2003), *vacated and remanded on other grounds*, 123 Fed. Appx. 21 (2d Cir. 2005) (citing with approval *McGarry's, Inc. v. Rose*; remanding for consideration of Fifth Amendment claim).

6. Fifth Amendment privilege

A person summoned to answer questions from an IRS agent is entitled to assert the Fifth Amendment right not to testify against oneself, where appropriate. The assertion of the privilege, however, is subject to the same limitations that obtain in other situations. "The witness is not exonerated from answering merely because he declares that in so doing he would incriminate himself   his say-so does not of itself establish the hazard of incrimination. It is for the court to say whether his silence is justified." *Hoffman v. United States*, 341 U.S. 479, 486 (1951); *accord Fisher v. United States*, 425 U.S. 391, 410 (1976). "It is well established that the privilege

Pulliam, 557 F.2d 426 (5th Cir. 1977).

protects against real dangers, not remote and speculative possibilities." *Zicarelli v. New Jersey State Comm'n*, 406 U.S. 472, 478 (1972); *see also Kastigar v. United States*, 406 U.S. 441, 444-45 (1972) (holding that the Fifth Amendment "protects against any disclosures which the witness reasonably believes could be used in a criminal prosecution or could lead to other evidence that might be so used").

As a corollary to this principle, "a mere blanket assertion of the privilege will not suffice." *United States v. Hatchett*, 862 F.2d 1249, 1251 (6th Cir. 1988). The privilege must be asserted with specificity. If the summoned party appears at a compliance hearing, but is not given the opportunity to invoke the privilege on a question-by-question basis because no relevant and specific questions were asked, he will not have relinquished the privilege. It is thus "incumbent upon the Government to ask specific questions" when a summoned party does appear. *United States v. Drollinger*, 80 F.3d 389, 393 n.5 (9th Cir. 1996) (failure to appear at enforcement hearing and at contempt hearing and to appeal either the enforcement or the contempt order did not waive the privilege). If the agent excuses appearance based on a blanket assertion of the Fifth Amendment, the IRS may be found to have waived compliance thereby rendering the summons unenforceable. *See United States v. Malnik*, 489 F.2d 682 (5th Cir. 1974); *United States v. Lipshy*, 492 F. Supp. 35, 39 (N.D. Tex. 1979).

Some courts will conduct their own in camera examination to determine whether the privilege has been properly asserted question by question. *United States v. Argomaniz*, 925 F.2d 1349, 1355 (11th Cir. 1991). Courts may provide the summoned party an opportunity to assert the privilege even after it has enforced the summons. *United States v. Allee,* 888 F.2d 208 (1st Cir. 1989).

a. Act of Production

A person who invokes the Fifth Amendment as a basis to withhold documents must "make a showing as to how disclosure of the summoned documents might tend to incriminate him." *United States v. Fox*, 721 F.2d 32, 40 (2d Cir. 1983). The act of producing evidence in certain circumstances may violate an individual's Fifth Amendment rights. *Fisher*, 425 U.S. at 410-13. This is so because the act of complying with the Government's request may have testimonial aspects and an incriminating effect. *See United States v. Doe*, 465 U.S. 605, 612 (1984). By producing summoned documents, the taxpayer may tacitly concede "the existence of the papers demanded and their possession or control by the taxpayer," and he may authenticate the documents by indicating his "belief that the papers are those described in the" summons. *Fisher*, 425 U.S. at 410. *See United States v. Hubbell*, 530 U.S. 27, 41-43 (2000) (holding that because the grand jury subpoena was so broad, the respondent had to "make extensive use of 'the contents of his own mind'" in order to identify the responsive documents, and the act of producing the documents therefore had a testimonial aspect) (citation omitted).

Where the existence, possession and authenticity of the summoned documents are established as "foregone conclusion[s]," the summoned party's act of producing the documents "adds little or nothing to the sum total of the Government's information," and does not "rise[] to the level of testimony within the protection of the Fifth Amendment." *Fisher*, 425 U.S. at 411; *Doe*, 465 U.S. at 614 n.13. As explained in *Fisher*, 425 U.S. at 411 (quoting *In re Harris*, 221 U.S. 274, 279 (1911)), "[u]nder these circumstances . . . '[t]he question is not of testimony but of surrender.'" *See United States v. Norwood*, 420 F.3d 888, 895-896 (8th Cir. 2005) (existence of documents associated with credit card accounts a "foregone conclusion"); *see also United States v. Teeple*, 286 F.3d 1047, 1049 (8th Cir. 2002); *United States v. Stone*, 976 F.2d 909, 911-12 (4th Cir. 1992); *United States v. Rue*, 819 F.2d 1488, 1492 (8th Cir. 1987).

b. Collective entity doctrine

There is a critical distinction between collective entities and individuals, when it comes to the Fifth Amendment. It is well established that an individual cannot rely on his Fifth Amendment privilege against compulsory self-incrimination to avoid producing the records of a collective entity which are in his possession in a representative capacity. *Braswell v. United States*, 487 U.S. 99, 104 (1988); *Bellis v. United States*, 417 U.S. 85, 88 (1974); *In re Grand Jury Proceedings*, 771 F.2d 143, 148 (6th Cir. 1985) (en banc). While this rule was first announced with respect to corporate records, it also applies to other collective entities including dissolved corporations, partnerships, labor unions and other unincorporated associations. *Bellis*, 417 U.S. at 88-89. This rule also applies to former officers of a corporation. *In re Grand Jury Subpoena Dated Nov. 12, 1991*, 957 F.2d 807, 812 (11th Cir. 1992) ("We hold that a custodian of corporate records continues to hold them in a representative capacity even after his employment is terminated. It is the immutable character of the records as corporate which requires their production and which dictates that they are held in a representative capacity. Thus, the production of such documents is required regardless of whether the custodian is still associated with the corporation or other collective entity."). *But see In re Three Grand Jury Subpoenas Duces Tecum Dated Jan. 29, 1999*, 191 F.3d 173 (2d Cir. 1999); *In re Grand Jury Subpoena Duces Tecum Dated June 13, 1983 & June 22, 1983*, 722 F.2d 981 (2d Cir. 1983).

c. Required records exception

The "required records" exception to the Fifth Amendment applies to the disclosure of documents which persons in a regulated industry are required by the Government to maintain. *See generally In re Grand Jury Proceedings*, 601 F.2d 162, 168 (5th Cir. 1979). There are several reasons for this rule, notably that "the public interest in obtaining such information outweighs the private interest opposing disclosure and the further rationale that such records become tantamount to public records." *Id.* (internal citations omitted). Additionally, courts have held that production of such records is "in a sense consented to as a condition of being able to carry on the regulated activity involved." *Id.* at 171.

The Supreme Court first recognized the required records exception in *Shapiro v. United States*, 335 U.S. 1 (1948), and formulated the standards for the exception in *Grosso v. United States*, 390 U.S. 62, 67-68 (1968):

> The premises of the doctrine, as it is described in *Shapiro,* are evidently three: first, the purposes of the United States' inquiry must be essentially regulatory; second, information is to be obtained by requiring the preservation of records of a kind which the regulated party has customarily kept; and third, the records themselves must have assumed "public aspects" which render them at least analogous to public documents.

This formulation of the rule has become a three-part test that courts generally apply to determine whether the required records exception applies. *See generally In re Grand Jury Subpoena*, 21 F.3d 226, 228 (8th Cir. 1994).

The required records exception is distinguishable from the "collective entity doctrine," which holds that collective entities such as corporations have no Fifth Amendment protection. *See generally In re Grand Jury Subpoena Dated Nov. 12, 1991*, 957 F.2d at 810. Although sole proprietors are not subject to the collective entity doctrine and may otherwise have Fifth Amendment rights, they are subject to the required records exception. *See In re Grand Jury Subpoena*, 21 F.3d at 230; *see also In re Grand Jury Subpoena Duces Tecum Served upon Underhill*, 781 F.2d 64, 67-70 (6th Cir. 1986) (applying required records exception to sole proprietorships); *Bionic Auto Parts & Sales, Inc. v. Fahner*, 721 F.2d 1072, 1082 (7th Cir. 1983); *Herman v. Galvin*, 40 F. Supp. 2d 27, 29 (D. Mass. 1999).

Courts have held that the required records exception applies to income tax return preparers who are compelled by Section 6107(b) to retain and disclose tax returns. *See United States v. Nordbrock*, 65 A.F.T.R.2d (RIA) 660, 662 (D. Ariz. 1990), *rev'd on other grounds* 941 F.2d 947 (9th Cir. 1991); *United States v. Bohonnon*, 628 F. Supp 1026, 1028-29 (D. Conn.), *aff'd without opinion,* 795 F.2d 79 (2d Cir. 1985). But at least one circuit has refused to apply the exception to records required by Section 6001. *United States v. Porter*, 711 F.2d 1397, 1404-05 (7th Cir. 1983).

7. Non-possession

When an IRS summons is served, the rights and obligations of the party on whom the summons was served become fixed. *United States v. Darwin Constr. Co.,* 873 F.2d 750, 755 (4th Cir. 1989). Receipt of a summons imposes a duty to retain possession of the documents pending a judicial determination of the enforceability of the summons. *United States v. Asay*, 614 F.2d 655, 660 (9th Cir. 1980).

If the respondent did not have possession or control of the documents at the time the summons was served, he must raise this as a defense to enforcement of the summons in the initial enforcement proceeding. *United States v. Rylander*, 460 U.S. 752, 757 (1983). Lack of possession or control of the requested records is a defense to the enforcement of a summons only if the respondent properly establishes non-possession. *Id.* The Government is not required to make any showing that the requested books and documents are within the possession or control of the respondent. On the contrary, the respondent bears the burden of producing credible evidence of non-possession. *See United States v. Lawn Builders of New England, Inc.*, 856 F.2d 388, 392 (1st Cir. 1988) (stating that the court "rejected the contention that the IRS must *prove by positive evidence* the existence of the records and their possession by the summonee") (emphasis in original) (citing *United States v. Freedom Church*, 613 F.2d 316, 322 (1st Cir. 1979); *United States v. Huckaby*, 776 F.2d 564, 567 (5th Cir. 1985) (a defendant must prove a lack of possession by the introduction of "credible evidence"); *United States v. Graber*, 81

A.F.T.R.2d (RIA) 429 (8th Cir. 1998). Thus, if the respondent wishes to raise a defense of non-possession, he must present credible evidence that he does not have possession or control of the requested documents.

Not possessing the records is not a defense to enforcement of the summons if the respondent caused the records to not be in his possession after receiving the summons. *Asay*, 614 F.2d at 660. "Not surprisingly, the law does not allow a custodian of records to send them away after receiving a summons and then claim he cannot produce them because they are no longer in his possession." *United States v. Three Crows Corp.*, 324 F. Supp. 2d 203, 206 (D. Me. 2004).

The Fifth Amendment may not be invoked as a substitute for evidence proving that the records are not in the respondent's possession. The Fifth Amendment privilege "has never been thought to be in itself a substitute for evidence that would assist in meeting a burden of production." *Rylander*, 460 U.S. at 758. The Supreme Court analogized to a criminal defendant's right against self-incrimination: "That the defendant faces such a dilemma demanding a choice between complete silence and presenting a defense has never been thought an invasion of the privilege against compelled self-incrimination." *Id.* at 759 (emphasis omitted). If the Fifth Amendment were permitted to replace the burden to produce evidence, it "would convert the privilege from the shield against compulsory self-incrimination which it was intended to be into a sword whereby a claimant asserting the privilege would be freed from adducing proof in support of a burden which would otherwise have been his." *Id.* at 758. Just as a defendant in a criminal trial is required to produce evidence of any defense he wishes to raise, so too must the respondent produce credible evidence of non-possession if he wishes to raise it as a defense to enforcement.

Often the taxpayer first asserts non-possession in a contempt proceeding following the taxpayer's failure to comply with an enforcement order. However, once a court orders enforcement of the summons, a presumption arises that the documents are in existence and in the continuing possession and control of the respondent. *United States v. Sorrells*, 877 F.2d 346, 348 (5th Cir. 1989). *See also United States v. Roberts*, 858 F.2d 698, 701 (11th Cir. 1988) (court's enforcement order is res judicata on the issue of possession at the time when the order was entered). Because parties may not relitigate the merits of the original court order at a contempt proceeding, taxpayers may not avoid contempt by arguing that the documents were not in their possession prior to enforcement. *Rylander*, 460 U.S. at 757; *Lawn Builders of New England, Inc.,* 856 F.2d at 395. However, the respondent may raise a *present* inability to comply as a defense to entry of an order of contempt. "While the court is bound by the enforcement order, it will not be blind to evidence that compliance is now factually impossible." *Rylander,* 460 U.S. at 757. A taxpayer claiming present inability to comply with the summons has the burden of production with respect to that impossibility. *Id. See also United States v. Drollinger*, 80 F.3d 389, 393 (9th Cir. 1996); *United States v. Sorrells*, 877 F.2d at 349. Self-serving denials by the respondent are not sufficient to meet this burden. *Roberts*, 858 F.2d at 701. The respondent must show that he undertook "in good faith all reasonable efforts to comply." *United States v. Rizzo*, 539 F.2d 458, 465 (5th Cir. 1976).

8.   Improper purpose or institutional bad faith

Taxpayers may argue that the IRS summons was issued for an improper purpose by alleging that the IRS acted in bad faith in issuing the summons, issued the summons to harass the taxpayer, or that the IRS is pressuring the taxpayer to settle a collateral dispute.

A court must look at the "institutional posture" of the IRS and determine whether the summons was issued with the intent to harass the taxpayer. *United States v. LaSalle Nat'l Bank*, 437 U.S. 298, 316 (1978). In *United States v. Millman*, 822 F.2d 305 (2d Cir. 1987), the Second Circuit further explained the "institutional posture" test:

> [T]he "institutional posture" test is the appropriate standard for determining whether a summons is issued merely to harass the taxpayer, that the motive of an agent involved in an investigation is a relevant factor in determining that institutional posture, as are the particular facts of each investigation and each taxpayer's situation, and that while the institutional test is applicable to a claim such a Millman's, how that posture, and the good faith of the IRS, are determined is a matter for case-by-case adjudication.

Id. at 309. While the personal intent of the agent is relevant, it is not dispositive. *LaSalle Nat'l Bank,* 437 U.S. at 316. The taxpayer must disprove the *actual* existence of a valid purpose by the IRS in issuing the summons. "After all, the purpose of the good-faith inquiry is to determine whether the agency is honestly pursuing the goals of § 7602 by issuing the summons." *Id.*

The taxpayer cannot meet this burden if he or she makes mere conclusory allegations without specific facts showing an improper purpose. *LaSalle,* 437 U.S. at 316. In responding to the Government's showing, the taxpayer must factually oppose the Government's allegations by affidavit. Legal conclusions or mere memoranda of law will not suffice. *United States v. Garden State Nat'l Bank,* 607 F.2d 61, 71 (3d Cir. 1979) (conclusory allegations are insufficient). If the taxpayer meets his burden, he may be provided an opportunity to substantiate his or her claims in a limited evidentiary hearing. (*See* Section III.C.)

Although the following list of cases is not exclusive, it illustrates various arguments that a taxpayer might make regarding the impropriety of the Government in attempting to enforce the summons:

- Summons issued to harass taxpayers: *United States v. Cmty. Fed. Sav. & Loan Ass'n,* 661 F.2d 694 (8th Cir. 1981); *United States v. Cecil E. Lucas Gen. Contractor, Inc.,* 406 F. Supp. 1267 (D.S.C. 1975).

- Improper ex parte communications between the IRS Appeals Office and the Examination Division: *Robert v. United States,* 364 F.3d 988 (8th Cir. 2004) (even though the court found that the ex parte communications were improper, the summonses were enforced because the improper communications did not evidence bad faith or an improper purpose in issuing the summonses).

- The summonses allegedly were issued to retaliate against the taxpayers for exercising their rights to free association, free speech, and substantive and procedural due process. *United States v. Kis,* 658 F.2d 526, 539 (7th Cir. 1981).

- The IRS might improperly disclose the summoned documents: *United States v. Barrett,* 837 F.2d 1341 (5th Cir. 1988) (holding that the district court may not conditionally enforce a summons to prevent violations of I.R.C. § 6103); *United States v. Jose,* 131 F.3d 1325, 1328 (9th Cir. 1997) (en banc) (reversing the district court's order requiring the IRS to notify the taxpayer before distributing the summoned documents to other divisions of the IRS, including CI).

- IRS committed fraud in gathering information used to issue the summons: *United States v. Deak-Perera & Co.*, 566 F. Supp. 1398, 1402 (D.D.C. 1983).

- Summons used to skirt discovery rules: *PAA Mgmt., Ltd. v. United States*, 962 F.2d 212 (2d Cir. 1992); *United States v. Admin. Co.*, 74 A.F.T.R.2d (RIA) 5252 (N.D. Ill. 1994) (holding that where summonses were issued before Tax Court petition is filed, there is no abuse of Tax Court's discovery rules).

- Information used to prepare summons came from illegal wiretap: *United States v. Millstone Enters., Inc.*, 864 F.2d 21 (3d Cir. 1988) (holding that district court erred in considering whether summons was based on illegal wiretap at contempt hearing).

9. Criminal referral

Taxpayers occasionally complain that a civil summons was issued in bad faith because the IRS was attempting to collect information by which it can bring criminal charges. The possibility that criminal charges could be considered at some time in the future does not make the summons invalid. *Donaldson v. United States*, 400 U.S. 517, 544 (1971). Indeed, a summons may be issued in furtherance of a criminal investigation. Prior to 1982, the IRS summons power could be exercised only if there was a civil purpose to the examination, but the enactment of I.R.C. § 7602(b) changed that. Now, a summons may be issued solely in furtherance of a criminal investigation, provided that the matter has not yet been referred to the Department of Justice for review and prosecution. *(See* Section II(B)(2)(b).)

10. Intervening events

In general, the validity of a summons is tested as of the date of issuance and events occurring after the date of issuance, but before enforcement, should not affect enforceability. *See Garpeg, Ltd. v. United States*, 583 F. Supp. 799 (S.D.N.Y. 1984) (subsequent referral to the Department of Justice for criminal prosecution); *PAA Mgmt., Ltd. v. United States*, 962 F.2d 212, 219 (2d Cir. 1992) (filing of Tax Court petition after issuance of summons); *United States v. Admin. Enters., Inc.*, 46 F.3d 670 (7th Cir. 1995) (passage of time since issuance of summons).

There are two notable exceptions to the general rule: First, compliance with the summons before enforcement is ordered will, in most cases, obviate the need for an enforcement order. However, compliance by the summoned person after an enforcement order is issued will not moot an appeal of an enforcement order or of the denial of a petition to quash the summons. *Church of Scientology v. United States,* 506 U.S. 9, 17-18 & n. 11 (1992).

Second, an enforcement action cannot be commenced after a "Department of Justice referral" (as defined in Internal Revenue Code section 7602(d)) has been made. This prohibition applies as well to seeking enforcement in response to a petition to quash, as is permitted by Section 7609(b)(2)(A). *DeGroote v. United States,* 57 A.F.T.R.2d (RIA) 1373 (W.D.N.Y. 1986).

D. SPECIALTY SUMMONSES

1. John Doe summonses

John Doe summonses are issued to discover the identities of unknown taxpayers. All proceedings involving such summonses are handled by the Tax Division. The Tax Division's current policy is that a Deputy Assistant Attorney General for the Tax Division should approve the filing of a petition seeking authorization to serve a John Doe summons. *(See Section III.E.)*

In *United States v. Bisceglia,* 420 U.S. 141 (1975), the Supreme Court held that Sections 7601 and 7602 of the Internal Revenue Code empowered the IRS to issue John Doe summonses to discover the identity of unknown taxpayers. Congress subsequently codified this authority in Section 7609(f), which requires that, before the IRS may serve a John Doe summons, it must obtain authorization from a federal district court judge in an ex parte court proceeding.

At the ex parte court proceeding, the Government must establish (1) that the summons relates to the investigation of a particular person or ascertainable group or class of persons; (2) that there is a reasonable basis for believing that such person or group or class of persons may fail or may have failed to comply with any provision of any internal revenue law; and (3) that the information sought to be obtained from the examination of the records or testimony (and the identity of the person or persons with respect to whose liability the summons is issued) is not readily available from other sources.

I.R.C. § 7609(f). *See In re Does*, 671 F.2d 977 (6th Cir. 1982); *see also United States v. Pittsburgh Trade Exch., Inc.*, 644 F.2d 302, 306 (3d Cir. 1981); *United States v. Brigham Young Univ.*, 679 F.2d 1345, 1349-50 (10th Cir. 1982) *rev'd on other ground*, 459 U.S. 1095 (1983); *United States v. Kersting*, 891 F.2d 1407, 1409 (9th Cir. 1989).

If the summoned party refuses to comply with a John Doe summons, the Government can pursue enforcement by filing a petition with the federal district court in which the summoned party resides or is found. The traditional *Powell* factors also apply to enforcement of a John Doe summons. Pursuant to Section 7609(e)(2), the running of the statute of limitations with respect to the John Doe is suspended, if compliance with the John Doe summons is not resolved within six months after service of the summons.

2. Summons for records from a church (I.R.C. § 7611)

Special rules apply when issuing and seeking enforcement of a summons issued as part of an examination of a church. All proceedings involving the enforcement of such summonses are to be handled by the Tax Division. As a matter of practice, a Deputy Assistant Attorney General and the appropriate Section Chief should be notified whenever a suit to enforce a summons in connection with an examination of a church has been received by the Tax Division.

Section 7611 imposes procedural and substantive requirements on the IRS's ability to examine the tax exempt status of a church and whether any of its activities may be subject to tax. The term "church" includes any organization claiming to be a church and any convention or association of churches. I.R.C. § 7611(h)(1); Treas. Reg. § 301.7611-1, Q&A3.

The statute requires that before the IRS may even inquire, a "high-level Treasury official" must reasonably believe, based on facts and circumstances recorded in writing, that the church may not be exempt or that it is carrying on an unrelated trade or business that is subject to tax or may have engaged in activities that are subject to tax. It is important to make sure that the person making this determination has been properly delegated this responsibility. Once the high-level official forms the required belief, a church is entitled to written notice of and the basis for the belief.

In order to begin a church tax examination, in addition to the notice of inquiry, a notice of examination must be sent to the church, with a copy to Division Counsel/Associate Chief Counsel, Tax Exempt and Government Entities, describing the records and activities which the IRS seeks to examine. The notice must describe the IRS's concerns and include copies of all relevant documents which would be disclosable if a FOIA request had been made. In addition, the notice must provide an opportunity for a conference with the IRS. Any examination must be completed within two years from the date of the notice of examination. This period will be suspended under certain circumstances, including any period during which a summons enforcement proceeding is pending.

Church records may be examined *only*, "to the extent necessary" to determine liability for and amount of tax. Religious activities may be examined *only* "to the extent necessary" to determine whether an organization claiming to be a church is a church for any period. Accordingly, in addition to the *Powell* requirements, the Government's papers must demonstrate "necessity," which requires a particularized showing of need for each category of records summoned. *United States v. C.E. Hobbs Found. for Religious Training & Educ., Inc.*, 7 F.3d 169 (9th Cir. 1993); *United States v. Church of Scientology Western U.S.*, 973 F.2d 715 (9th Cir. 1992); *United States v. Church of Scientology of Boston, Inc.*, 933 F.2d 1074 (1st Cir. 1991).

3. Summons for computer software (I.R.C. § 7612)

Computer software, particularly the underlying source code, may be valuable intellectual property that often contains copyrighted material or trade secrets. *See United States v. Norwest Corp.* 116 F.3d 1227 (8th Cir. 1997); *United States v. Caltex Petroleum Corp.*, 12 F. Supp. 2d 545 (N.D. Tex. 1998). Congress has specified the circumstances under which the IRS may summon and use software and source code. I.R.C. § 7612. Section 7612 has two important parts: (1) protection for the confidentiality of all executable software; and (2) special rules for summoning the source code of tax related software.

"Computer software executable code" is "any object code, machine code, or other code readable by a computer when loaded into its memory and used directly by such computer to execute instructions." I.R.C. § 7612(d)(3)(A). Section 7612 protects the confidentiality of executable software by (1) giving courts jurisdiction to enter protective orders for software; and (2) imposing conditions on the use of software that comes into possession of the IRS, notwithstanding the terms of any protective order. The conditions include limiting access to the software to specific IRS personnel identified to the taxpayer, limiting use of the software to the audit at hand, returning the software at the end of the audit, and agreeing not to disclose information learned about the software. Additionally, § 7612(c)(2)(H) makes it clear that software shall be treated as return information for purposes of I.R.C. § 6103.

Section 7612 also details the circumstances under which the IRS can summon computer software source code. Source code is defined as a "code written by a programmer using a programming language which is comprehensible to appropriately trained persons and is not capable of directly being used to give instructions to a computer." I.R.C. § 7612(d)(2)(a). For purposes of § 7612, source code also includes programmer notes, design documents, memoranda, and similar documents, as well as related customer communications. I.R.C. §§ 7612 (d)(2)(B) & (C).

Before the IRS may issue a summons for source code, it must show that it is not able to ascertain the correctness of an item on the return by using the taxpayer's books, papers, records, or other data, or by using the executable version of the program (the version the taxpayer used). In this narrow circumstance, Congress has decided that the IRS is required to prove need before it can get the source code. Further, the IRS must identify, with specificity, the portion of the source code that is necessary to verify the correctness of an item on the return. Additionally, the Secretary or his delegate must make a determination that the need for the source code outweighs the risks of unauthorized disclosure of trade secrets.

There are exceptions to these requirements for criminal investigations, source code acquired or developed for internal use rather than being available for commercial distribution, any communications between the software owner and the taxpayer, and any tax-related computer source code that is required to be produced by some other section of the Code. I.R.C. § 7612(b)(2).

4. Summons pursuant to Tax Treaty and Tax Information Exchange

The IRS may exercise its summons authority to carry out any obligations of the United States under a bilateral tax treaty or tax information exchange agreement (TIEA) with the United States. A TIEA allows both parties to obtain from each other information that "may be necessary or appropriate to carry out and enforce the[ir] tax laws." I.R.C. § 274(h)(6)(C)(i). The United States is party to more than 50 bilateral tax treaties and 15 bilateral TIEAs which can be used by either the United States or its treaty partner to obtain documents and testimony located in the other party's territory for criminal and civil tax investigations and proceedings. These pacts are concluded by the United States Department of Treasury, with the assistance of the IRS and the Tax Division of the Department of Justice, and are administered by the Director, International, Large and Mid-Size Business Division, IRS, as the Competent Authority for the United States.

When a treaty partner makes a request to the United States under one of these pacts, the Office of the Competent Authority refers the matter to either a revenue agent or special agent in the field where the evidence is located, and directs the agent to undertake the execution of the request. The agent will attempt to obtain the requested information by asking the witness(es) or record holder(s) in question to provide such information voluntarily, but, if the information cannot be obtained voluntarily, the agent will issue summons(es) on behalf of the treaty partner to obtain the requested information.

The Tax Division typically conducts such litigation arising from a summons issued on behalf of a treaty partner in much the same way as it would with respect to an IRS summons issued for a domestic tax investigation. This summary procedure has been explicitly approved in the context of an IRS summons issued in furtherance of the Government's obligations under a tax treaty or TIEA. *United States v. Stuart*, 489 U.S. 353 (1989); *Barquero v. United States*, 18 F.3d 1311, 1316 (5th Cir. 1994). To obtain enforcement of a treaty partner summons, the IRS must establish the four *Powell* factors. While the IRS must establish its good faith in issuing the summons, the IRS does not have to attest to   much less prove   the good faith of the requesting nation. *Mazurek v. United States,* 271 F.3d 226, 231 (5th Cir. 2001).

The Government makes a prima facie showing for enforcement by submitting, in addition to the declaration of the IRS agent who issued the summons, the declaration of the U.S. Competent Authority responsible for administering the tax treaty in question. *Stuart*, 489 U.S. at 360; *Barquero*, 18 F.3d at 1316-17.

The Competent Authority's declaration should include a description of the duties and responsibilities of the Competent Authority (*i.e.*, administering all exchange of information programs under tax treaties and exchange of information agreements) and the identification and description of the foreign request. In general, the Competent Authority should aver that:

(1) the summons was issued and served in response to a request by a foreign government;

(2) the Competent Authority personally reviewed the request;

(3) the Competent Authority determined that the request is properly within the scope of the tax treaty in question;

(4) the Competent Authority determined that it is appropriate for the United States to give assistance to the foreign country in question pursuant to the request;

(5) the foreign tax authorities have reason to believe that the subject of the foreign tax inquiry may have failed to comply with the foreign country's tax laws during the periods covered by the summons;

(6) the requested information is not within the possession of the IRS or the foreign authorities;

(7) the requested information may be relevant to a determination of the foreign subject's tax liability;

(8) the same type of information can be obtained by the foreign tax authorities under the foreign country's tax laws;

(9) it is the understanding of the parties to the tax treaty in question that information exchanged will only be used by the applicant State for the purposes identified in the tax treaty;

(10) exchanged information may only be disclosed as required in the normal administrative or judicial process operative in the administration of the tax system of the applicant State; and

(11) improper use of the information would be protested and, if continued, would lead to recommendations to terminate the tax treaty.

An attorney to whom a treaty-partner summons is assigned may obtain the declaration of the Competent Authority by contacting Branch 7, Associate Chief Counsel (International), IRS. That office may also provide advice and other forms of assistance for the conduct of the litigation.

5. Designated summonses (I.R.C. § 6503(j))

Designated summonses are very rare. All proceedings involving such summonses are handled by the Tax Division.

Examinations of large corporations may warrant the application of a team examination approach and the examination may qualify as a "Coordinated Industry Case" (CIC). *See* I.R.M. §§ 4.45.1.2, *et seq.*[9] Designated summonses are only issued in connection with a CIC. I.R.M. § 25.5.3.3(2); I.R.C. § 6503 (j)(1). Often in CIC exams, taxpayers will agree to extend the statute of limitations on assessment in order to permit the IRS to complete the audit and obtains the information it needs by asking for the information through information document requests (IDR's). However, on occasion, a CIC taxpayer will decline to voluntarily produce information the IRS agents need to complete the audit, and will also decline to voluntarily extend the statute of limitations. In such circumstances the IRS can unilaterally extend the statute of limitations on assessment by issuing a designated summons and seeking judicial enforcement of that summons (or related summonses issued within thirty days of the issuance of the designated summons). This helps explain why designated summons cases are often contentious   the IRS is holding the statute of limitations open when the taxpayer does not want the statute extended.

A designated summons must meet three specific requirements:

(1) Prior to issuance, a designated summonses must be reviewed by Area Counsel of the Office of Chief Counsel, for the region where the examination is being conducted. I.R.C. § 6503(j)(2)(A)(i);[10]

(2) A designated summons must be issued at least 60 days before the statute of limitations will expire (including any extensions the taxpayer has agreed to. I.R.C. § 6503(j)(2)(A)(ii);

(3) And the summons must specifically state on its face that it is a designated summons. I.R.C. § 6503(j)(2)(A)(iii).

The standard for enforcement of a designated summons is the *Powell* standard. It is not necessary for the IRS to make any showing that the

---

[9] Before the 1998 IRS reorganization, the CIC program was called the coordinated examination program (CEP). CIC is the successor to CEP.

[10] This statutory requirement was added after the decision in *United States v. Derr*, 968 F. 2d 943 (9th Cir. 1992), which held that the examining agent had the authority to issue a designated summons.

taxpayer had been uncooperative in the audit prior to the issuance of the summons. *United States v. Derr,* 968 F.2d 943 (9th Cir. 1992).

The IRS may only issue one designated summons per return. However, the IRS may issue other summonses within the 30-day period beginning when the designated summons is issued that relate to the same return which also will hold the statute of limitations open during the judicial enforcement period. I.R.C. § 6503(j)(1)(A)(ii).

The designated summons does not itself toll the running of the statute of limitations. If the designated summons or a related summons is enforced, the statute of limitations remains suspended for 120 days after the end of the judicial enforcement period. I.R.C. § 6503 (j)(1)(B). If the designated summons is not enforced, the statute remains open for 60 days after the close of the judicial enforcement period.

The IRS must seek judicial enforcement of the designated or related summonses before the statute of limitations expires. If it does so, the statute of limitations is suspended during the judicial enforcement period, which is defined as the period beginning of the day the proceeding to enforce the summons is brought and ending on the day on which there is a "final resolution" as to the summoned person's response to each summons. I.R.C. § 6503(j)(3).

The term "final resolution" of the summoned person's response to such summons is not defined by statute. The IRS has issued proposed regulations dealing with this question. Prop. Treas. Reg. § 20.8199-91, 68 Fed. Reg. 44905-01 (2003), *reprinted in* 2003-2 C.B. 756. The proposed regulations, relying on the legislative history, assert that the term "final resolution" in the context of a designated summons is the same as it is under I.R.C. § 7609 (e)(2)(B), namely that no court proceedings remain pending, the period for appeal has run, and the summoned party has fully complied with the summons to the extent ordered by the court. If all appeal periods have expired but the summoned party has not complied with the summons to the extent required by the court order, the proposed regulations provide that final resolution does not occur until the summoned party has complied with the summons to the extent of the court order.

However, because designated summonses are issued in connection with the audit of large corporate returns, the summoned information is often voluminous and complex. Therefore, it is not always the case that the IRS agents will be able to immediately determine that the taxpayer has fully complied. The proposed regulations deal with this problem by stating that the determination of compliance will be made as soon as practicable, and that notice of the determination shall be made in writing within five days. If the taxpayer is not satisfied with leaving this issue in the hands of the IRS, it may give the IRS a written statement of compliance that requests the IRS issue a determination that the taxpayer has fully complied with the summons. If the taxpayer files a statement of compliance within 180 days of receipt of the statement, the IRS must notify the taxpayer by certified mail that the IRS is not satisfied with the taxpayer's compliance. If the IRS does not issue such a notice, the summons will be deemed to have been complied with as of the 180th day after the statement of compliance was received.

III. PROCEDURES

A. PETITION TO ENFORCE

1. Which office should file

The United States Attorneys Manual §§ 6-5.210 and 6-5.221 provide that, in general, IRS Chief Counsel attorneys may directly refer to the United States Attorneys routine requests to enforce summonses and to defend petitions to quash. Cases involving sensitive or novel issues should be referred to and are to be handled by the Tax Division. The manual provides that Tax Division attorneys are to handle cases involving summonses issued to or for:

- attorneys
- churches
- newspapers and newspaper reporters
- tax accrual workpapers (tax pool analysis)
- foreign document requests
- treaty partners or other matters with international implications
- John Doe summonses
- Section 6050I
- novel/complex Fifth Amendment claims
- computer software and other non-traditional items
- state/local agencies and courts
- designated summonses

- consent directives
- Sections 6700 and 6701
- Sections 6707 and 6708
- other unique issues as may be determined from time to time.

Among the issues that the Tax Division has determined it should handle are all summons proceedings involving examinations of promoters of:

- tax shelters,
- scams,
- and schemes.
- In addition, the Division handles all summons proceedings arising from the Offshore Credit Card Project when the summons involves a request for offshore records.

The Chief of the appropriate Civil Trial Section should be notified immediately of all adverse decisions. All appeals, whether initiated by the United States or the other party, will be handled by the Appellate Section of the Tax Division. U.S.A.M. § 6-5.230. If you have any questions, please contact the Chief of the appropriate Civil Trial Section:

- Civil Trial Section, Central, Seth G. Heald, Chief

- Civil Trial Section, Northern, Patrick D. Mullarkey, Chief

- Civil Trial Section, Eastern, David A. Hubbert, Chief

- Civil Trial Section, Southern, Michael J. Kearns, Chief

- Civil Trial Section, Southwestern, Louise P. Hytken, Chief

- Civil Trial Section, Western, Richard R. Ward, Chief

2. Approvals

Proceedings to enforce certain types of summonses must be approved by higher level officials at the Tax Division:

- Summonses to attorneys and law firms must be approved by the Assistant Attorney General, Tax Division.

- "John Doe" summonses must be approved by the Deputy Assistant Attorney General, Tax Division.

- Summonses to the press or media for information other than purely financial records unrelated to the news gathering function (*e.g.,* employment records of an employee of a newspaper) must be approved by the Attorney General. A request for such approval should be submitted through the Deputy Assistant Attorney General and Assistant Attorney General of the Tax Division.

3. Documents to File

Documents for submission may vary from court to court. Consult local rules and practice to determine what is needed in your jurisdiction.

Documents for submission to the court to enforce a summons generally include (1) petition, (2) declaration, and (3) proposed order to show cause. The attached forms provide suggested language, but they should be tailored to fit the requirements of the local jurisdictions.

The petition *[Exhibit 2]* provides the jurisdictional grounds for the suit, asserts the underlying facts, and provides a request for relief. Fed. R. Civ. P. 8. It also demonstrates satisfaction of the relevant legal standards and tests.

The agent issuing and serving the summons is generally the one signing the declaration *[Exhibit 3]* for submission with the petition. It is a sworn statement putting forward the relevant facts in the case. If the IRS provides an agent declaration with the request to enforce, the assigned attorney should review it carefully to assure that it satisfies all requirements necessary to enforcement and does not contain any extraneous recitations. Moreover, the attorney should review any declaration with the agent, even if it has already been signed, to assure that it is still accurate and complete. Even though establishing a prima facie case for enforcement through an agent's declaration "isn't much of a hurdle," *2121 Arlington Heights Corp. v. IRS*, 109 F.3d 1221, 1224 (7th Cir. 1997), attorneys should take care to present persuasive support for enforcement through the declarations. A well-drafted declaration should anticipate defenses to enforcement.

The typical proposed show cause order *[Exhibit 4]* either sets the time and date for a hearing or provides a place for the court to do so. It also includes a finding that the *Powell* factors have been met, and sets deadlines for any response.

The order to show cause, when approved by the judge, represents a determination that the United States has made a prima facie showing that the *Powell* requirements have been satisfied and, consequently, shifts the burden to the summoned person to demonstrate or "show cause" why the summons should not be enforced. In order for the court to obtain personal jurisdiction over the summoned person, the summoned person must be served with the order to show cause. *See United States v. Gilleran*, 992 F.2d 232, 233 (9th Cir. 1993) ("The district court acquires personal jurisdiction over the taxpayer by service of the show cause order and the petition for enforcement of the summons."); *United States v. Miller*, 609 F.2d 336, 338 (8th Cir. 1979) (service of summons and complaint not required, as "[t]he district court predicated personal jurisdiction on the service of the show cause order and the petition for enforcement" on respondent); *United States v. McCarthy*, 514 F.2d 368, 372 (3d Cir. 1975) ("Process on the complaint could be in the form of an order served on the person summoned fixing a deadline for filing any responsive pleading, albeit an informal pleading, together with an affidavit, and any motions, and directing that person to show cause at a date and time certain why an order should not be entered enforcing the administrative summons. The order should provide that unless the court determines otherwise, any motions and issues raised by the pleadings will be considered at the return date of the order to show cause.").

4. Service of order to show cause

After the court issues the order to show cause, it must be served on the summoned party. Service of process other than a district court summons or a subpoena is governed by Fed. R. Civ. P. 4.1, which provides for service by the "United States marshal, or a person specially appointed for that purpose, who shall make proof of service as provided in Rule 4(l)." Accordingly, the proposed order to show cause presented to court should provide that service may be made by any agent, officer, or other person designated by the IRS. A copy of the petition, declaration, and any other document submitted to the court in support of the petition must be served on the summoned party along with the order to show cause. The proposed order to show cause should provide for the method(s) of service and may propose alternative service methods for the court's consideration. The person making service should complete a proof of service provided by the trial attorney or Assistant United States Attorney.

5. Monitoring compliance

As soon as an order requiring compliance of a summons is received, the attorney should forward it to the issuing agent with a request to be informed whether there has been compliance. Under ordinary circumstances, the issuing agent will receive the summoned documents and testimony. The attorney should remain available to the agent to facilitate compliance. The case file is not ready to be closed until the summoned party has complied.

6. Contempt procedures

An attorney assigned to a summons enforcement case should monitor the case to assure full compliance with any enforcement order. If a party has not fully complied with the summons, the attorney should attempt to confer with the party to determine if the party will comply without additional judicial action. Once the attorney determines that the party will not comply, the attorney should file a motion to find the respondent in contempt.

The motion should identify the order of the court (the summons enforcement order) with which the respondent failed to comply, and should detail the respondent's noncompliance. The motion for contempt should be supported with a declaration from the agent setting forth that respondent was aware of the order and that respondent failed to comply with the order. The motion for contempt is generally accompanied by a proposed order to show cause why respondent should not be held in contempt, which sets a hearing date for further court action.

At any hearing on contempt, the attorney should be prepared to address any issues the respondent may raise for failing to comply, such as current non-possession of the information, or the Fifth Amendment. The attorney should also be prepared to address possible coercive sanctions for non-compliance, including fines and incarceration.

B. RESPONDING TO PETITIONS TO QUASH

When a petition to quash a summons is filed, the Government should file an appropriate response as soon as possible. The response may take the form of a motion to dismiss for lack of jurisdiction, a motion for summary denial, a counterclaim for enforcement, or something similar in accordance with local practice.

The Government may, but is not obligated to, file a counter-petition or motion to enforce the summons. (*See* Section II(B)(4)(b)). The United States may simply move to dismiss the petition to quash pursuant to Fed. R. Civ. P. 12(b)(6). *See Cosme v. Internal Revenue Service*, 708 F.Supp. 45, 48 (E.D.N.Y. 1989); *Tarpley v. United States*, 1997 WL 767577, *1 (S.D.N.Y. Dec 11, 1997). If the United States files a motion to dismiss without simultaneously seeking an order enforcing the summons, the United States need not establish a *Powell* prima facie case; rather "'the burden shifts immediately to the petitioner to establish a valid defense to the summons.'" *Knauss v. United States*, 28 F.Supp.2d 1252, 1254 (S.D.Fla. 1998) (quoting *Cosme*, 708 F.Supp. at 48); *Conrad v. United States*, 1989 WL 165576, *1 (W.D.Mich. Nov 09, 1989); *Deleeuw v. I.R.S.*, 681 F.Supp. 402 (E.D.Mich. 1987); *Jungles v. United States*, 634 F.Supp. 585, 586 (N.D.Ill.1986).

A declaration from the agent or office is necessary if filing a counterclaim for enforcement, and may be appropriate to rebut allegations asserted in the petition to quash. It is important to respond as quickly as possible so that the IRS's examination is not unduly delayed.

C. DISCOVERY AND EVIDENTIARY HEARINGS

Most summons enforcement proceedings should be decided on the papers, except for the very rare case where the party opposing enforcement has established the existence of a question as to a material fact. Discovery thus is rarely appropriate in summons proceedings, and evidentiary hearings are also rare.

1. Limitations on discovery

The summary nature of summons proceedings limits the circumstances under which discovery is available. *United States v. Stuart*, 489 U.S. 353, 369 (1989) (quoting S. Rep. No. 97-494, vol. 1, at 285 (1982), *reprinted in* 1982

U.S.C.C.A.N. 781, 1031. Discovery is rarely appropriate in summons cases. *See United States v. Kis*, 658 F.2d 526, 540 (7th Cir. 1981); *Chen Chi Wang v. United States*, 757 F.2d 1000, 1004 (9th Cir. 1985); *United States v. Will*, 671 F.2d 963, 967-68 (6th Cir. 1982). In order for discovery to occur, a taxpayer must make "a substantial preliminary showing that enforcement of the summons would result in an abuse of the court's process" and that "discovery would likely lead to useful, relevant evidence." *Robert v. United States*, 364 F.3d 988, 999-1000 (8th Cir. 2004).

When respondents seek an opportunity to propound formal discovery requests they often have the real and improper objective of trying to shift the court's focus from the *Powell* standard to a critique of the IRS's investigative techniques. This is not a proper inquiry for a summons enforcement proceeding. *Tiffany Fine Arts, Inc. v. United States*, 469 U.S. 310, 323 (1985). "[I]t is for the agency, and not the taxpayer, to determine the course and conduct of an audit, and 'the judiciary should not go beyond the requirements of the statute and force IRS to litigate the reasonableness of its investigative procedures.'" *United States v. Norwest Corp.*, 116 F.3d 1227, 1233 (8th Cir. 1997) (quoting *United States v. Clement*, 668 F.2d 1010, 1013 (8th Cir. 1982)).

Sometimes respondents couch their requests for discovery in terms of seeking to determine whether the summons was issued for an improper purpose. The Court in *Powell* clearly did not intend to permit taxpayers to use the "improper purpose" exception as a pretext for litigating the wisdom of the IRS's investigatory techniques. The mere allegation of improper purpose is not sufficient to justify discovery. *See United States v. Ladd*, 471 F. Supp. 1150, 1153 n.3 (N.D. Tex. 1979) (no prehearing discovery when taxpayer failed "to include circumstances upon which her claim of improper purpose was based"). When the purported purpose of a discovery request is to inquire into the motivation for an audit, the movant must show "extraordinary circumstances" that set them apart from any other taxpayer. *United States v. Judicial Watch, Inc.*, 371 F.3d 824, 830-31 (D.C. Cir. 2004) (quoting *SEC v. McGoff,* 647 F.2d 185, 193 (D.C. Cir. 1981)).

Indeed, some courts have held that they will not decide whether discovery should be allowed until after an evidentiary hearing is held. *United States v. Harris*, 628 F.2d 875, 882 (5th Cir. 1980) (citing with approval *United States v. Salter*, 432 F.2d 697 (1st Cir. 1970) (discovery should be allowed in summons enforcement proceedings only after the court has heard cross-examination of agent at the evidentiary hearing and determines that further discovery is necessary); *United States v. McCarthy,* 514 F.2d 368 (3d Cir. 1975); *United States v. Church of Scientology*, 520 F.2d 818 (9th Cir. 1975); *United States v. Abrahams*, 905 F.2d 1276 (9th Cir. 1990); *United States v. Lask,* 703 F.2d 293 (8th Cir. 1983); *Kis,* 658 F.2d at 542.

2.   Evidentiary Hearings

Summons enforcement proceedings are intended to be summary in nature with the sole purpose of insuring "that the IRS has issued the summons for a proper purpose and in good faith." *United States v. BDO Seidman*, 337 F.3d 802, 810 (7th Cir. 2003). Because summonses are issued during the investigative stage, no guilt or liability on the part of the taxpayer need be established. "The summons power 'is not a power to procure or perpetuate evidence at all; it is strictly inquisitorial.'" *PAA Mgmt., Ltd. v. United States,* 962 F.2d 212, 219 (2d Cir. 1992) (citation omitted). *See also United States v. Mueller,* 930 F.2d 10, 12 (8th Cir. 1991) (taxpayer "could not use the proceedings to enforce the IRS summons as a forum in which to contest the validity of the underlying assessments"). Accordingly, "the enforcement proceeding should be concluded expeditiously so that the actual investigation can be continued." *Barrett,* 837 F.2d at 1349. "[C]ourts have recognized that a proceeding to enforce a tax summons is a most appropriate candidate for streamlined procedures." *United States v. McCoy,* 954 F.2d 1000, 1004 (5th Cir. 1992).

While a district court may, in its discretion, allow the taxpayer an evidentiary hearing to substantiate his allegations and supplement offers of proof that the summons was not issued in good faith, the "right to an adversary hearing . . . is not absolute." *United States v. Harris,* 628 F.2d 875, 879 (5th Cir. 1980). "There is no requirement that the court conduct [an evidentiary] hearing or permit discovery in each and every case. . . . [A] party challenging IRS summonses will be entitled to an adversary hearing only upon the production of some substantive evidence corroborating the claim of abuse." *Hintze v. IRS,* 879 F.2d 121, 126-27 (4th Cir. 1989). *See also United States v. BDO Seidman,* 337 F.3d 802, 809 (7th Cir. 2003); *Fortney v. United States*, 59 F.3d 117, 121 (9th Cir. 1995); *Copp v. United States,* 968 F.2d 1435, 1438 n.1 (1st Cir. 1992); *Alphin v. United States,* 809 F.2d 236, 238 (4th Cir. 1987); *United States v. Balanced Fin. Mgmt., Inc.,* 769 F.2d 1440, 1444 (10th Cir. 1985); *United States v. Tiffany Fine Arts, Inc.,* 718 F.2d 7, 14 (2d Cir. 1983), *aff'd,* 469 U.S. 310 (1985); *United States v. Kis,* 658 F.2d 526, 539 n.39 (7th

Cir. 1981); *United States v. Nat'l Bank of South Dakota*, 622 F.2d 365, 367 (8th Cir. 1980).

D. THE ROLE OF MAGISTRATE JUDGES

A magistrate judge does not have authority to render a final decision in a summons case. A magistrate judge's powers are enumerated in Section 636(a) of Title 28, and include procedural pretrial matters. Magistrate judges do not have authority to make a final determination on motions for judgment on the pleadings, for summary judgment, or other dispositive motions. 28 U.S.C. § 636(b)(1)(a). A summons proceeding is not a procedural pre-trial motion, and the respondent in a summons enforcement proceeding or petitioner who seeks to quash a summons is entitled to a determination by an Article III judge. *See Peretz v. United States*, 501 U.S. 923, 930-32 (1991). A summons enforcement order is a final dispositive and appealable order, *Reisman v. Caplin,* 375 U.S. 440, 449 (1964), beyond the authority of a magistrate judge to issue. *United States v. First Nat'l Bank,* 628 F.2d 871, 873 (5th Cir. 1980); *United States v. Wisnowski*, 580 F.2d 149 (5th Cir. 1978).

Proceedings may be conducted by a magistrate judge with the consent of both parties. While reference to a magistrate judge for report and recommendation, with a de novo determination by a district judge, satisfies the constitutional requirements, a final decision by a magistrate judge absent consent of the parties, does not. *See Flournoy v. Marshall*, 842 F.2d 875, 878 (6th Cir. 1988); *Fowler v. Jones*, 899 F.2d 1088, 1093 (11th Cir. 1990). An appeal from an "order" issued by a magistrate judge, absent consent of the parties, enforcing a summons will be subject to dismissal on the grounds that the order is not final. *United States v. Jones,* 581 F.2d 816, 817 (10th Cir. 1978). *See also Colorado Bldg. & Constr. Trades Council v. B.B. Andersen Constr. Co.,* 879 F.2d 809, 811 (10th Cir. 1989). When a magistrate judge mistakenly issues an "order" or "decision" rather than a report and recommendation, the attorney should ask the district judge to construe the magistrate judge's ruling as a report and recommendation that the district court enter an order enforcing the summons.

E. "JOHN DOE" SUMMONS PROCEDURES

A "John Doe" summons may be served only with judicial approval. I.R.C. § 7609(f). These cases are always handled by the Tax Division, and the

Deputy Assistant Attorney General, Tax Division, should approve the suit before it is filed.

Similar to a suit to enforce a summons, a suit seeking authorization to serve a John Doe summons is initiated by filing a petition and a declaration. The forms included in this manual contain suggested language. They may require modification to conform with local rules and practices.

A petition *[Exhibit 9]* provides the jurisdictional grounds for the suit, asserts the underlying facts, and provides a request for relief. Fed. R. Civ. P. 8. It also demonstrates satisfaction of the statutory requirements of § 7609(f).

A declaration *[Exhibit 10]* must be submitted with the petition. It is a sworn statement putting forward the facts that establish the criteria necessary for a court to approve service of the summons: (1) that the summons relates to the investigation of a particular person or ascertainable group or class of persons; (2) that there is a reasonable basis for believing that such person or group or class of persons may fail or may have failed to comply with any provision of any internal revenue law; and (3) that the information sought to be obtained from the examination of the records or testimony (and the identity of the person or persons with respect to whose liability the summons is issued) is not readily available from other sources. I.R.C. § 7609(f).

A proceeding seeking the court's authorization to serve a John Doe summons is ex parte. Thus, the matter is ripe for the court's consideration as soon as it is filed. Filing a notice *[Exhibit 13]* calling that fact to the attention of the court is recommended.

Finally, a proposed order *[Exhibit 12]* should be submitted for the court's execution.

F. APPEAL PROCEDURES

All appeals in summons cases   whether or not adverse   will be handled by the Appellate Section of the Tax Division. Exceptions to this policy must be approved by the Assistant Attorney General of the Tax Division. *See* U.S.A.M. § 6-5.230.[11]

If the court does not fully enforce the summons, the order is considered adverse. The Chief of the appropriate Civil Trial Section should be notified of adverse summons-related decisions as soon as practicable. *Id.*

- Civil Trial Section, Central, Seth G. Heald, Chief

- Civil Trial Section, Northern, Patrick D. Mullarkey, Chief

- Civil Trial Section, Eastern, David A. Hubbert, Chief

- Civil Trial Section, Southern, Michael J. Kearns, Chief

- Civil Trial Section, Southwestern, Louise P. Hytken, Chief

- Civil Trial Section, Western, Richard R. Ward, Chief

When a case is decided in favor of the Government, the United States Attorney should furnish the Tax Division with a copy of a notice of appeal or cross-appeal filed by an adverse party as soon as possible (preferably within 5 days of the filing of the notice). *See* U.S.A.M. § 6-5.700.[12] DOJ trial attorneys should consult with their managers to ensure than the correct actions and procedures are taken.

---

[11] http://www.usdoj.gov/usao/eousa/foia reading room/usam/title6/5mtax. htm#6-5.230

[12] http://www.usdoj.gov/usao/eousa/foia reading room/usam/title6/5mtax. htm#6-5.700

May 2006

IV. FORMS

CHECKLIST

✓	Requirement	Reference
	When seeking Enforcement. . .	
	• Is the correct office handling the case?	III.A.1
	• Is special approval required?	III.A.2
	• File in the district where the summoned party "resides or is found."	II.B.4.a.
	• Have the *Powell* Requirements been met?	
	• The summons was issued for a legitimate purpose?	II.B.2.a.(1)
	• The summoned information may be relevant?	II.B.2.a.(2)
	• The summoned information is not already in possession of the IRS?	II.B.2.a.(3)
	• All administrative requirements have been met?	II.B.2.a.(4)
	• Summons was properly issued?	
	• Summons was properly served?	
	• Summons copy was attested?	
	• Notification to taxpayer proper for third-party recordkeeper summons?	
	• No Justice Department referral in effect?	II.B.2.b.
	• Is the declaration complete and accurate?	
	• Are the factual allegations of the petition supported by the declaration?	
	• Have you reviewed the declaration with the agent?	
	When responding to a petition to quash . . .	II.B.4.
	• Was petition to quash timely filed?	
	• Was notice properly given?	
	• Was it filed in the district where the summoned party "resides or is found?"	
	• Was service on the United States proper?	

		Should the government file a cross-motion for enforcement ?	

UNITED STATES DISTRICT COURT

_____ DISTRICT OF_____

_____ DIVISION

UNITED STATES OF AMERICA,

Petitioner,

v.

Case No. _____

_____

Respondent.

PETITION TO ENFORCE IRS SUMMONS

The United States of America petitions this Court for an order enforcing the IRS

administrative summons served on the respondent, _____. In support, the United

States avers as follows:

1. Jurisdiction over this matter is conferred upon this Court by 26 U.S.C. §§ 7402 and 7604(a)

   and by 28 U.S.C. §§ 1340 and 1345.

2. The summoned person [persons] resides or may be found within the boundaries of this

   district.

3. _____is a Revenue Agent/ Revenue Officer/ Special Agent of the Internal Revenue

   Service, employed in the _____ Division of the IRS in _____.

4. Revenue Agent/ Revenue Officer/ Special Agent _____ is conducting an

   examination/investigation for the purpose of [determining the correct federal

   _____tax liabilities of _____for the periods _____]

   [collecting the assessed, unpaid federal _____ tax liabilities of _____ for the periods

_____] [determining whether respondents committed any offense connected with the administration or enforcement of the internal revenue law].

5. In his capacity as an IRS Revenue Agent/ Revenue Officer/ Special Agent _____ is authorized to issue IRS summonses pursuant to 26 U.S.C. § 7602, 26 C.F.R. § 301.7602-1, 26 C.F.R. § 301.7602-1T, and Internal Revenue Service Delegation Order No. 4 (as revised).

6. Pursuant to the above-described investigation, on _____, Revenue Agent/ Revenue Officer/ Special Agent _____ issued an IRS administrative summons to _____ directing _____ to appear before Revenue Agent/ Revenue Officer/ Special Agent _____ on _____ at ___ a.m./p.m., at the place identified in the summons. The summons directed _____ to appear and to give testimony and produce for examination certain books, papers, records, or other data as described in the summons.

7. Revenue Agent/ Revenue Officer/ Special Agent _____ served an attested copy of the summons [by delivering in hand to _____] [by leaving it at the last and usual place of abode of the person to whom it was directed] [by delivering in hand to _____, an officer of _____] [by certified mail].

8. The respondent failed to appear on _____, and, to date, has failed to comply with the summons.

9. [Except for the documents indicated in Revenue Agent/ Revenue Officer/ Special Agent _____'s declaration] [T]he testimony and documents described in the summons are not already in the possession of the IRS. [The United States does not seek enforcement of the summons with respect to those documents already within the IRS's possession.]

10. All administrative steps required by the Internal Revenue Code for the issuance of the IRS summons have been followed.

11. The testimony, books, records, papers, and/or other data sought by the summons may be relevant to the IRS's investigation.

12. No Justice Department referral is in effect within the meaning of 26 U.S.C. § 7602(d)(2) with respect to _____ for the years under investigation.

13. In order to obtain enforcement of a summons, the United States must establish that the summons: (1) is issued for a legitimate purpose; (2) seeks information relevant to that purpose; (3) seeks information that is not already within the IRS's possession; and (4) satisfies all administrative steps required by the Internal Revenue Code. *United States v. Powell*, 379 U.S. 48, 57-58 (1964).

14. The attached Declaration of Revenue Agent/ Revenue Officer/ Special Agent _____ establishes the government's prima facie showing under *Powell*.

WHEREFORE, the United States respectfully prays as follows:

A. That this Court enter an order directing the respondent to show cause in writing, if any, why he/she/it should not comply with and obey the aforementioned IRS summons and every requirement thereof;

B. That this Court enter an order directing the respondent to fully obey the subject summons and each requirement thereof, by ordering the attendance, testimony, and production required and called for by the terms of the summons, before Revenue Agent/ Revenue Officer/ Special Agent _____, or any other proper officer or employee of the IRS, at such time and place as may be set by Revenue Agent/ Revenue Officer/ Special Agent or any other proper officer or employee of the IRS;

C.   That the United States recover its costs incurred in maintaining this proceeding; and

D.   That the Court grant such other and further relief as the Court deems proper or justice may require.

Respectfully submitted this___ day of_____, ____.

_____
United States Attorney

By: _____

UNITED STATES DISTRICT COURT
_____ DISTRICT OF _____
_____ DIVISION

UNITED STATES OF AMERICA,

    Petitioner,

      v.   Case No. _____

_____,

    Respondent.

DECLARATION OF REVENUE AGENT/ REVENUE OFFICER/ SPECIAL AGENT _____

    I, _____ declare:

1.   I am a duly commissioned Revenue Agent/ Revenue Officer/ Special Agent employed in the

_____ of the Internal Revenue Service [with a post of duty at

_____]. Pursuant to 26 U.S.C. § 7602, 26 C.F.R. § 301.7602-1, 26 C.F.R.

§ 301.7602-1T, and Internal Revenue Service Delegation Order No. 4 (as revised), I am

authorized to issue administrative summonses.

2.   [_____is not my real name. It is a pseudonym I use in my official

capacity as an employee of the IRS. This pseudonym   used for privacy and safety

reasons   has been registered with the IRS, in accordance with IRS procedures (Internal

Revenue Manual 1.2.4), and all IRS procedures governing the use of pseudonyms have been

followed.]

3.   [Except where noted to the contrary, I have personal knowledge of the matters set forth in

this Declaration, and, if called upon to testify to such matters, could do so competently.]

4. In my capacity as a Revenue Agent/ Revenue Officer/ Special Agent, I am conducting an

    examination/investigation for the purpose of [determining the correct federal

    _____tax liabilities of _____for the periods _____]

    [collecting the assessed, unpaid federal _____ tax liabilities of _____ for the periods

    _____] [determining whether respondents committed any offense

    connected with the administration or enforcement of the internal revenue law].

5. *Describe nexus between examination/investigation and the summoned records.*

6. On _____in furtherance of my investigation, I issued an IRS

    administrative summons to _____. The summons directed _____ to appear at __

    a.m/p.m. on_____, to give testimony and produce for examination certain books,

    papers, records, or other data as described in the summons. A copy of the summons is

    attached as Exhibit A.

7. In accordance with 26 U.S.C. § 7603, [I served] [At my direction _____ served]

    an attested copy of the summons directed to _____[by delivering in hand to

    _____] [by leaving it at the last and usual place of abode of the person to whom it

    was directed] [by delivering in hand to _____, an officer of _____] [by

    certified mail]. A true and correct copy of the certificate of service is included as a part of

    Exhibit A.

8. The respondent failed to appear at the appointed time and, to date, has failed to comply with

    the summons.

9. [Attached to this declaration as Exhibit B is a list of the documents the IRS has obtained and

    those which it still seeks. With the exception of the specific documents indicated in Exhibit

B as already received,] [T]he books, records, papers and other data sought by the summons are not already in the possession of the Internal Revenue Service.]

10. The testimony, books, records, papers, and/or other data sought by the summons may be relevant to this investigation. *Explain why.*

11. No Justice Department referral, as defined by 26 U.S.C. § 7602(d)(2), is in effect with respect to _____ for the years under investigation.

12. All administrative steps required by the Internal Revenue Code for issuance of the summons have been followed.

I declare under penalty of perjury that the foregoing is true and correct.

Executed this ____ day of _____, ____.

_____
Revenue Agent/ Revenue Officer/ Special Agent
Internal Revenue Service

UNITED STATES DISTRICT COURT
_____ DISTRICT OF _____
_____DIVISION

UNITED STATES OF AMERICA,

    Petitioner,

    v.   Case No. _____

,

    Respondent/s.

ORDER TO SHOW CAUSE

Upon the petition of the United States and the Declaration of Revenue Agent

_____, including the exhibits attached thereto, it is hereby

ORDERED that the respondent/s, _____appear before the Honorable

_____, in that Judge's courtroom in the United States Courthouse,

_____on the _____ day of _____, ____, at _____

__.m., to show cause why _____ should not be compelled to obey the Internal

Revenue Service summonses served upon _____.

It is further ORDERED that:

1.   A copy of this Order, together with the petition and its exhibits, shall be served in

accordance with Rule 4(e) [(h)] of the Federal Rules of Civil Procedure upon the respondent/s

within [21] days of the date that this Order is served upon counsel for the United States or as soon

thereafter as possible. Pursuant to Rule 4.1(a), the Court hereby appoints Revenue Agent/

Revenue Officer/ Special Agent _____, or any other person designated by the IRS to

effect service in this case.

2.   Proof of any service done pursuant to paragraph 1, above, shall be filed with the Clerk as soon as practicable.

3.   Because the file in this case reflects a prima facie showing that the investigation is being conducted for a legitimate purpose, that the inquiries may be relevant to that purpose, that the information sought is not already within the Commissioner's possession, and that the administrative steps required by the Internal Revenue Code have been substantially followed, the burden of coming forward has shifted to the respondents to oppose enforcement of the summonses.

4.   If the respondent/s has/have any defense to present or opposition to the petition, such defense or opposition shall be made in writing and filed with the Clerk and copies served on counsel for the United States, at least [14] days prior to the date set for the show cause hearing. The United States may file a reply memorandum to any opposition at least 5 days prior to the date set for the show cause hearing.

5.   At the show cause hearing, only those issues brought into controversy by the responsive pleadings and factual allegations supported by affidavit will be considered. Any uncontested allegation in the petition will be considered admitted.

6.   Respondents may notify the Court, in a writing filed with the Clerk and served on counsel for the United States at the address(es) on the petition, at least [14] days prior to the date set for the show cause hearing, that the respondents have no objection to enforcement of the summonses. The respondents' appearance at the hearing will then be excused.

The respondents are hereby notified that a failure to comply with this Order may subject them to sanctions for contempt of court.

DONE and ORDERED at _____, _____this _____ day of

_____, _____.

_____
UNITED STATES DISTRICT JUDGE

UNITED STATES DISTRICT COURT
_____ DISTRICT OF _____
_____ DIVISION

UNITED STATES OF AMERICA,
    Petitioner,

      v.   Case No. _____

_____

Respondent.

CERTIFICATE OF SERVICE

The undersigned hereby certifies under penalty of perjury that he or she is an employee of

the Internal Revenue Service, is not a party to this action, and is a person of such age and

discretion as to be competent to serve papers.

    On _____ day of _____, _____, I served a copy of the below-listed papers

upon _____, by

(check and complete one)

    _____ Hand-delivering a copy to _____, at _____

    _____

    _____   Leaving a copy of each pleading at the respondent's dwelling house or usual

                place of abode with a person of suitable age and discretion then residing therein.

                Name of person with whom the summons and complaint were left: _____

                _____.

Papers served:

1) Order to Show Cause Re: Enforcement of Internal Revenue Summonses;

2) United States' Petition to Enforce an Internal Revenue Service Summonses;

3) Declaration of Revenue Agent ____.

I certify under penalty of perjury that the foregoing is true and correct.

Executed: _____   _____
                Date   Signature

IN THE UNITED STATES DISTRICT COURT FOR THE

_____ DISTRICT OF _____

_____ DIVISION

_____,)	
)	
Petitioner__,)	
)	
v.)	CIVIL ACTION NO. _____
)	
UNITED STATES OF AMERICA,)	
)	
Respondent.)	

MOTION TO DISMISS

The respondent, the United States of America, by its attorney, _____, and

pursuant to Rule 12(b) of the Federal Rules of Civil Procedure moves the Court for the entry of

an Order dismissing the above-titled action on the grounds that the commencement and

maintenance of the action is barred by the sovereign immunity of the United States; that the Court

lacks subject matter jurisdiction to entertain the proceeding; and that it fails to state a claim for

which relief may be granted.

A memorandum in support of this motion is filed and served concurrently herewith.

United States Attorney

By: _____
        Trial Attorney, Tax Division
        U.S. Department of Justice
        Post Office Box ____
        Ben Franklin Station
        Washington, D.C. 20044
        Telephone: (202) ____

CERTIFICATE OF SERVICE

IT IS HEREBY CERTIFIED that service of the above Motion has this _____ day of

_____, 20_, been effected upon petitioner__ by depositing a copy in the United

States mail at Washington, D.C., postage paid, addressed to petitioner(s)as follows, and

_____

[Additionally, as a courtesy, and for informational purposes only, [a] copy(ies) of the above

[was/were] mailed to the summoned person__ at the address set forth on [each of] the

summons__.]

IN THE UNITED STATES DISTRICT COURT FOR THE

_____ DISTRICT OF _____

_____ DIVISION

_____,	)
	)
Petitioner__,	)
	)
v.	) CIVIL ACTION NO._____
	)
UNITED STATES OF AMERICA,	)
	)
Respondent.	)
	)

RESPONDENT'S MEMORANDUM IN SUPPORT OF
MOTION TO DISMISS PETITION TO QUASH

The above-titled action has been brought by _____ seeking to quash _____

Internal Revenue Service summons__ issued to "_____."

The respondent, United States of America, has moved to dismiss the petition on the grounds

that the action is barred by the doctrine of sovereign immunity, that the Court lacks jurisdiction to

entertain the proceeding, and that it fails to state a claim for which relief may be granted.

QUESTIONS PRESENTED

1.   Whether the Court lacks jurisdiction to entertain a petition to quash [a] summons__

issued to [a] person__ who [is/are] not [a] third-party.

2.   *[Formulate questions appropriate to the case.]*

INTRODUCTION

Sections 7602 through 7609 of the Internal Revenue Code govern the procedure applicable

to issuance, compliance, enforcement, and challenges of summonses. Section 7602 is a broad grant of authority that applies to all summonses issued as part of an investigation of tax liability. *See United States v. Euge*, 444 U.S. 707, 714 (1980); *United States v. Arthur Young & Co.*, 465 U.S. 805, 816 (1984). Section 7609 is a detailed description of the procedures which apply to, and rights created by, issuance of a special category of summonses   third-party summonses. One entitled to receive notice of a third-party summons may bring a proceeding to quash the summons.

The "proceeding to quash" procedure, first enacted in 1982 as part of the Tax Equity and Fiscal Responsibility Act (TEFRA), was intended to provide some assurance that taxpayer interference with legitimate law enforcement efforts would be based on proper grounds and not merely interposed on frivolous grounds resulting in fruitless delays, as had frequently been the case before the passage of TEFRA. *See* S. Rep. No. 97-494, vol. 1, at 282, *reprinted in* 1982 U.S.C.C.A.N. 781, 1027; *Godwin v. United States*, 564 F. Supp. 1209, 1211-1212 (D. Del. 1983).

ARGUMENT

I

THE UNITED STATES HAS NOT WAIVED ITS SOVEREIGN IMMUNITY

Section 7609(b)(2), which allows a proceeding to quash an Internal Revenue Service summons to be brought against the United States constitutes a waiver of sovereign immunity. *See Stringer v. United States*, 776 F. 2d 274, 275 (11th Cir. 1985). Like all such waivers, the one contained in Section 7609 must be strictly construed. *See Lehman v. Nakshian*, 453 U.S. 156, 160 (1981); *Soriano v. United States*, 352 U.S. 270 (1957). "Men must turn square corners when they deal with the Government. If it attaches even purely formal conditions to its consent to be sued those conditions must be complied with." *Rock Island A. & L.R. Co. v. United States*, 254 U.S. 141, 143 (1920). These statutes are jurisdictional and limit the power of the federal courts to adjudicate claims against the United States. *F.D.I.C. v. Meyer,* 510 U.S. 471, 475 (1994) ("Sovereign immunity is jurisdictional in nature.").

Because Section 7609(b) is not applicable here [has not been complied with], and no other statute waives sovereign immunity for the instant suit, this Court lacks jurisdiction and the action should be dismissed. *[Insert discussion of 7609 requirements, as appropriate.]*

Petition Not Timely

One of the conditions of the United States' waiver of sovereign immunity is that a petition to quash must be commenced within 20 days of the date notice of the summons is given. Section 7609(b)(2)(A). Where, as here, the action was not commenced against the United States as prescribed by statute, the Court must dismiss the petition. *Berman v. United States,* 264 F.3d 16, 19 (1st Cir. 2001) (motion to quash must be filed within 20 days of mailing notice); *accord Faber v. United States,* 921 F.2d 1118 (10th Cir. 1990); *Stringer v. United States,* 776 F.2d 274 (11th Cir. 1985); *Ponsford v. United States,* 771 F.2d 1305, 1309 (9th Cir. 1985). Section 7609(b)(2)(A) provides, in part, "any person who is entitled to notice of a summons under subsection (a) shall have the right to begin a proceeding to quash such summons not later than the 20th day after the day such notice is given in the manner provided in subsection (a)(2)." Subsection (a)(2) of Section 7609 provides, "notice shall be sufficient if . . . such notice . . . is mailed by certified or registered mail to the last known address of such person. . . ." Thus, the date that notice of the summons was mailed begins the running of the 20-day period. *Shipley v. United States,* 74 A.F.T.R.2d 94-7713 (E.D. Cal. 1994); *Brohman v. United States,* 587 F. Supp. 62 (W.D.N.Y. 1984); *Riggs v. United States,* 575 F. Supp. 738 (N.D. Ill. 1983); *Grisham v. United States,* 578 F. Supp. 73 (S.D.N.Y. 1983); *Bilodeau v. United States,* 577 F. Supp. 234 (N.H. 1983).

The certificates of service and of notice on the summons__ demonstrate that proper notice was given on _____, in the manner as required by 26 U.S.C. Section 7609(a). This petition to quash was filed on _____, 200__, more than 20 days after notice was given. Accordingly, since the United States has not consented to be sued except as to suits filed "not later than the 20th day after such notice is given," sovereign immunity has not been waived and the petition should be dismissed.

Summons Out of District.

Section 7609(h)(1) provides that the district court in which the summoned person "resides or is found" shall have jurisdiction to entertain an otherwise proper petition to quash. This provision is a jurisdictional requirement rather than a matter of venue. *Deal v. United States*, 759 F.2d 442, 444 (5th Cir. 1985); *Fortney v. United States*, 59 F.3d 117, 119 (9th Cir. 1995). The Fifth Circuit stated that jurisdiction is "vested in the district where the summons is to be answered" rather than "by the location of the taxpayer." *Masat v. United States*, 745 F.2d 985, 988 (5th Cir. 1984). *See also, Beck v. United States*, 2003 WL 1194253, 91 A.F.T.R.2d 2003-1345 (6th Cir. 2003); *Oldham v. United States*, 89 A.F.T.R.2d (RIA) 2095, 2097 (D. Or. 2002) (the statute requires "something more than the Due Process analysis of minimum contacts" and requires "a physical presence within the forum").

In this case, the summoned person, _____, neither resides nor is found in this judicial district. *[Insert appropriate facts.]* Accordingly, the petition must be dismissed.

Section 7609 does not apply to the type of summons at issue in this case.

Section 7609(c) defines the types of summonses that can be challenged under 7609(b)(2) and expressly excepts certain summonses. Section 7609(b)(2) does not apply to any summons ["served on the person with respect to whom the summons is issued." § 7609(c)(2)(A).]

[issued in aid of collection. § 7609(c)(2)(D)]

["issued by a criminal investigator of the Internal Revenue Service in connection with the investigation of an offense connected with the administration or enforcement of the internal revenue laws; and served on any person who is not a third-party recordkeeper (as defined in section 7603((b))." § 7609(c)(2)(E). Section 7603(b)(2) provides that the following ten categories of persons are "third-party recordkeepers": (A) banks; (B) consumer reporting agencies; (C) persons extending credit through credit cards or other similar devices; (D) brokers; (E) attorneys; (F) accountants; (G) any barter exchange; (H) regulated investment companies and their agents; (I) enrolled agents; and (J) owner or developer of a computer software source code (as defined in section 7612(d)(2)).]

Failure to Comply with the Requirements of Section 7609(b)(2)(b).

Petitioner failed to comply with the requirement of Section 7609(b)(2)(B) to send a copy of the petition by registered or certified mail to both the summoned person and the issuing agent within 20 days after the IRS gave notice. *Dorsey v. United States*, 618 F. Supp. 471 (D. Md. 1985); *Yocum v. United States*, 586 F. Supp. 317 (N.D. Ind. 1984) (failure to give notice to Internal Revenue Service); *Fogelson v. United States*, 579 F. Supp. 573 (D. Kan. 1983) (oral notice to summoned party inadequate); *McTaggart v. United States*, 570 F. Supp. 547, 551 (E.D. Mich. 1983) (failure to give notice to summoned party).

II

THE PROVISIONS OF THE PRIVACY AND
FREEDOM OF INFORMATION ACTS DO NOT
APPLY TO IRS SUMMONSES

The government need not comply with either the Privacy Act, 5 U.S.C. § 552a, *et seq.*, or the Freedom of Information Act, 5 U.S.C. § 552, *et seq.*, as a prerequisite to issuing or enforcing a summons. *United States v. McAnlis*, 721 F. 2d 334, 337 (11th Cir. 1983); *Uhrig v. United States*, 592 F. Supp. 349, 353 (D. Md. 1984); *McTaggert v. United States*, 570 F. Supp. 547, 550 (E.D. Mich. 1983); *United States v. Will*, 475 F. Supp. 492, 494 (M.D. Fla. 1979). Neither act contains any provision which allows either the quashing or the denial of enforcement of an Internal Revenue Service summons as a remedy for any alleged failure to provide information or to maintain secrecy as required by those acts. Indeed, it would be inconsistent with the intent of Congress, which urges the speedy enforcement of summonses, if the Court were to allow such a challenge to the summons[es] to be maintained.

III

IMPROPER SERVICE

Fed. R. Civ. P. 4(i) provides that service upon the United States shall be effected by delivering a copy of the summons and complaint to the United States Attorney for the district in which the action is brought and by sending a copy of the summons and complaint to the Attorney General of the United States at Washington, D.C. In this case, *[state the facts in your case]*. Accordingly, unless the petitioners show a justifiable excuse for their failure to serve properly, the petition should be dismissed for insufficiency of service of process. See *Hart v. United States*, 817 F.2d 78, 80 (9th Cir. 1987).

Additionally, the petition should be dismissed based on Petitioners' failure to obtain issuance of a summons. As with a complaint, a petition to quash an IRS summons requires the issuance of a summons under Fed. R. Civ. P. 4. *See Kish v. United States*, 77 A.F.T.R.2d 96-1305, 1996 WL 196730, *1 (W.D.Mich. 1996); *see also* Fed. R. Civ. P. 4(b) and (c) (summons shall be issued for each defendant to be served and must be served together with a copy of the complaint). In this case, *[state the facts in your case]* . For this reason, the petition should be dismissed under Fed. R. Civ. P. 12(b)(4).

Petitioners may argue that they are entitled to a reasonable time to cure the defective service in this case under Fed. R. Civ. P. 4(i)(3). That rule is inapplicable, however. Rule 4(i)(3) applies only when the plaintiff must serve federal officers in addition to the U.S. Attorney and the Attorney General. *Tuke v. United States*, 76 F.3d 155, 158 (7th Cir. 1996). Even if the rule was applicable to this case, it entitles a plaintiff time to cure defective service only "if the plaintiff has served either the United States attorney or the Attorney General of the United States." Fed. R. Civ. P. 4(i)(3)(A). In this case, *[state the facts in your case]* . Therefore, Petitioners' case must be dismissed.

IV
PETITIONER FAILS TO STATE
A CLAIM FOR WHICH RELIEF CAN
BE GRANTED

The petitioner fails to set forth any allegations which would constitute a legally sufficient challenge or defense to the enforcement of the IRS summons.

[Identify and deal with objections raised in petition].

CONCLUSION

For the foregoing reasons the proceeding should be dismissed.

Respectfully submitted,

_____
United States Attorney

By: _____
Assistant United States Attorney

_____
Trial Attorney, Tax Division
U.S. Department of Justice
Post Office Box ____
Ben Franklin Station
Washington, D.C. 20044
Telephone: (202)_____

IN THE UNITED STATES DISTRICT COURT FOR THE

DISTRICT OF

DIVISION

	)	
	)	
Petitioner__,	)	
	)	
v.	)	CIVIL NO. _____
	)	
UNITED STATES OF AMERICA.	)	
	)	
Respondent__.	)	

ORDER OF DISMISSAL

This matter having been submitted to the Court on the motion of the United States to

dismiss the above-titled action to quash summons, the Court having considered the matter on the

papers pursuant to Rule 78 of the Federal Rules of Civil Procedure, and for good cause shown, it

is this _____ day of _____, 200__, hereby

ORDERED that the above-titled proceeding is dismissed [for the reason--].

DONE and ORDERED at _____, _____, this _____ day of _____,

200__.

_____
UNITED STATES DISTRICT JUDGE

UNITED STATES DISTRICT COURT
_____ DISTRICT OF_____
_____ DIVISION

IN THE MATTER OF THE TAX
LIABILITIES OF:

JOHN DOES, United States taxpayers who,
during [*tax period and identify group*]

**EX PARTE PETITION FOR LEAVE
TO SERVE "JOHN DOE" SUMMONS**

The United States of America avers as follows:

1.   This *ex parte* proceeding is commenced pursuant to Sections 7402(a), 7609(f), and

7609(h) of the Internal Revenue Code (26 U.S.C.), for leave to serve an Internal Revenue

Service "John Doe" summons upon _____.

2.   _____ is found at _____ within the jurisdiction of

this Court.

3.   As explained in the Declaration of Revenue Agent _____ attached as Exhibit

A, the Internal Revenue Service is conducting an investigation to determine the correct

federal _____ tax liabilities, for [periods] of United States taxpayers who [*describe

group*].

4.   In furtherance of this investigation, the Internal Revenue Service, [has issued] [once

service of the summons is authorized by the Court, will issue] under the authority of

Section 7602 of the Internal Revenue Code, an administrative "John Doe" summons

to_____. A copy of the summons is attached to the Exhibits Appendix to

Declaration of Revenue Agent_____ at Tab 1.

5.   The "John Doe" summons relates to the investigation of an ascertainable group or class of persons, that is, United States taxpayers who, [*describe group*]. There is a reasonable basis for believing that such group or class of persons may fail, or may have failed, to comply with one or more provisions of the Internal Revenue laws. The information sought to be obtained from the examination of the records or testimony (and the identity of the persons with respect to whose tax liabilities the summonses have been issued) is not readily available from other sources.

6.   In support of this Petition, the United States submits a Declaration of Revenue Agent

_____ attached as Exhibit A; the Exhibits Appendix to the Declaration

of Revenue Agent_____; and a Memorandum.

WHEREFORE, the United States respectfully requests:

A.   That this Court enter an order permitting service of an Internal Revenue Service

"John Doe" summons to _____ in substantially the form as attached to the

Exhibits Appendix to the Declaration of Revenue Agent _____at Tab 1; and

B.   That this Court grant such other and further relief as the Court deems proper or

justice may require.

_____

United States Attorney

By: _____

Trial Attorney, Tax Division
U.S. Department of Justice

UNITED STATES DISTRICT COURT
_____ DISTRICT OF_____
_____ DIVISION

IN THE MATTER OF THE TAX
LIABILITIES OF:

JOHN DOES, United States taxpayers who,
during [*tax period and identify group*]

DECLARATION OF _____

I, _____ pursuant to 28 U.S.C. Section 1746, declare and state:

\#   I am a Revenue Agent/Officer _____with the

_____Division of the Internal Revenue Service. I have been a Revenue

Agent/Officer for __ years. [*Describe specific relevant training and experience*]

\#   The Internal Revenue Service is conducting an investigation to determine the

correct federal tax liabilities, for [*periods*] of United States taxpayers who [*identify group*]

\#   To facilitate this investigation, the Internal Revenue Service, [*has issued*] [*once

authorized by the court, will issue*] under the authority of Section 7602 of the Internal Revenue

Code (26 U.S.C.), a "John Doe" summons to _____ and its affiliates and

subsidiaries. A copy of this summons is attached to the Exhibits Appendix, submitted

contemporaneously with this Declaration, at Tab 1.

\#   [*Describe the summoned party and records sought.*]   The records sought by the

summons will reveal the identities of and/or disclose transactions by persons who may be liable

for federal taxes and will enable the Internal Revenue Service to investigate whether those

persons have complied with the internal revenue laws.

\# Based on information received by the Internal Revenue Service, it is likely that a significant number of the persons who have

  [*Detail the basis for the belief that the "John Doe" class has failed, or may have failed, to comply with the internal revenue laws.*]

  [*Detail the history of the IRS's investigation of the class and how the information summoned may assist in that investigation.*]

\# The summons to _____ seeks to identify persons in the 'John Doe' class not yet identified. [*Give details*]

\# Based upon the foregoing, I have concluded the "John Doe" summons relates to the investigation of an ascertainable group or class of persons; there is a reasonable basis for believing that such group or class of persons may fail, or may have failed, to comply with one or more provisions of the Internal Revenue laws; and the information sought to be obtained from the examination of the records or testimony (and the identity of the persons with respect to whose tax liabilities the summonses have been issued) is not readily available from other sources.

  I declare under penalty of perjury, pursuant to 28 U.S.C. Section 1746, that the foregoing is true and correct.

  Executed this _____ day of _____

           _____

           Revenue Agent/Officer
           Internal Revenue Service

UNITED STATES DISTRICT COURT
_____ DISTRICT OF_____
_____ DIVISION

IN THE MATTER OF THE TAX
LIABILITIES OF:

JOHN DOES, United States taxpayers who,
during [*tax period and identify group*]

MEMORANDUM IN SUPPORT OF
EX PARTE PETITION FOR LEAVE
TO SERVE "JOHN DOE" SUMMONS

The United States of America respectfully submits the following Memorandum in

support of its *EX PARTE* PETITION FOR LEAVE TO SERVE JOHN DOE SUMMONS:

INTRODUCTION

This is an *ex parte* proceeding brought by the United States of America, pursuant to

Sections 7609(f) and (h) of the Internal Revenue Code (26 U.S.C.), for leave to serve an

Internal Revenue Service "John Doe" summons upon _____. Section 7609(f) provides

that a summons which does not identify the person with respect to whose liability it is issued

may be served only after a court proceeding in which the United States establishes certain

factors. These types of summonses are known as "John Doe" summonses. Section 7609(h)(1)

provides that a district court in which the person to be summoned resides or is found shall have

jurisdiction to hear and determine any proceeding brought under Section 7609(f). Section

7609(h)(2) provides that any determinations required to be made under Section 7609(f) shall be

made *ex parte* and shall be made solely on the petition and supporting affidavits.

QUESTIONS PRESENTED

Whether, as required by Section 7609(f), the United States of America has demonstrated (1) that the "John Doe" summons which the Internal Revenue Service desires to serve upon _____ relates to the investigation of an ascertainable group or class of persons; (2) that there is a reasonable basis for believing that such group or class of persons may fail or may have failed to comply with any provision of any internal revenue law; and (3) that the information sought to be obtained from the examination of the records or testimony (and the identities of the persons with respect to whose liability the summons is issued) is not readily available from other sources.

DISCUSSION

The Internal Revenue Service is conducting an investigation to determine the correct federal income tax liabilities, for the years ended _____, of United States taxpayers[13] who _____

In furtherance of this investigation, the United States is requesting authorization for the IRS to serve a "John Doe" summons on _____.

---

[13]The term "United States taxpayer" refers to all persons subject to tax in the United States. All United States citizens and resident aliens are liable for federal income taxes on income received from sources within or without the United States; nonresident aliens are only liable for taxes on income from sources within the United States. Pursuant to Section 7701(b)(1), an alien may be treated as a resident for the purposes of income taxation if he (1) is a lawful permanent resident of the United States, (2) meets the substantial presence test (this is an objective test in which the number of days the alien is present in the United States are counted), or (3) makes an election to be treated as a resident. *See Lujan v. Comm'r*, T.C. Memo 2000-365, 2000 WL 1772503 (2000).

I.   The Summons for Which the Government Seeks Authorization Meets the Requirements of a "John Doe" Summons

Section 7601 of the Internal Revenue Code requires the Secretary of the Treasury to "cause officers or employees of the Treasury Department to proceed, from time to time, through each internal revenue district and inquire after and concerning all persons therein who may be liable to pay any internal revenue tax." Section 7602 authorizes the Secretary to summon records and testimony for that purpose. Specifically, Section 7602 authorizes the Secretary "[f]or the purpose of ascertaining the correctness of any return, making a return where none has been made, [or] determining the liability of any person for any internal revenue tax . . . [t]o summon . . . any person having possession, custody, or care of books of account containing entries relating to the business of the person liable for tax . . ., or any other person the Secretary may deem proper, to appear . . . and to produce such books, papers, records, or other data, and to give such testimony, under oath, as may be relevant or material to such inquiry."

Section 7602 is the Internal Revenue Service's principal information-gathering authority, and, accordingly, the courts have broadly construed it in light of its intended purpose of furthering the effective conduct of tax investigations. Thus, the courts have repeatedly rejected attempts to circumscribe or thwart the effective exercise of the Internal Revenue Service's summons power. *See, e.g., United States v. Euge*, 444 U.S. 707, 715-716 (1980); *United States v. Bisceglia*, 420 U.S. 141 (1975); *Couch v. United States*, 409 U.S. 322, 338 (1973).

In *Bisceglia*, the Supreme Court held that Sections 7601 and 7602 empowered the Internal Revenue Service to issue a "John Doe" summons to a bank to discover the identity of a person who had engaged in certain bank transactions. This authority was subsequently codified in Section 7609(f) of the Internal Revenue Code, as added by the Tax Reform Act of 1976.

Section 7609(f) provides:

> Any summons . . . which does not identify the person with respect to whose liability the summons is issued may be served only after a court proceeding in which the Secretary establishes that
>
> > (1) the summons relates to the investigation of a particular person or ascertainable group or class of persons,
> >
> > (2) there is a reasonable basis for believing that such person or group or class of persons may fail or may have failed to comply with any provision of any internal revenue law, and
> >
> > (3) the information sought to be obtained from the examination of the records or testimony (and the identity of the person or persons with respect to whose liability the summons is issued) is not readily available from other sources.

The "John Doe" summons for which the United States seeks authorization in the instant case meets those three requirements.

A.   The Investigation Is Related to an Ascertainable Class

As required by Section 7609(f)(1), the group or class of persons to be investigated here is ascertainable   United States taxpayers _____ [describe ascertainable group or class]. Where the identities of the taxpayers are yet not known, no greater specificity can be expected in defining the group or class of persons.

B.   Reasonable Basis Exists for the Belief That the Unknown Persons May Fail, or May Have Failed to Comply with the Internal Revenue Laws

With respect to the second requirement, set forth in Section 7609(f)(2), the Declaration of Revenue _____ reflects a reasonable basis for believing that the unknown persons whose identities are sought by the summonses may fail, or may have failed, to comply with one or more provisions of the internal revenue laws.

First, _____ [describe transactions at issue] are inherently reasonably suggestive of tax avoidance, given that tax avoidance is frequently the purpose for _____. In *United States v. Pittsburgh Trade Exchange, Inc.*, 644 F.2d 302, 306 (3d Cir. 1981), the court held that the "reasonable basis" test had been met based upon a revenue agent's testimony that barter transactions of the type arranged by the Pittsburgh Trade Exchange were "inherently susceptible to tax error." In *United States v. Ritchie*, 15 F.3d 592, 601 (6th Cir. 1994), the court held that the mere payment for legal services with large amounts of cash is a reasonable basis for the issuance of a "John Doe" summons. Likewise, _____ provides a reasonable basis for the issuance of the summons at issue.

[add additional legal support such as law review articles, cases, statutes]

Second, the Declaration of Revenue Agent _____ [add factual support such as newspaper articles, webpages and information about litigation and prosecutions involving similarly situated taxpayers]. *See, e.g., United States v. Brigham Young University*, 679 F.2d 1345, 1349-50 (10th Cir. 1982), *vacated for consideration of mootness*, 459 U.S. 1095 (1983) (prior audit experience with other contributors that had overvalued "in kind" contributions was a reasonable basis for issuing a "John Doe" summons for the identity of all "in kind" contributors to Brigham Young University); *United States v. Kersting*, 891 F.2d 1407, 1409 (9th Cir. 1989) ("John Doe" summons enforced after district court found "the existence of at least one case in which a Tax Court found some of Kersting's programs to be abusive of the tax code."

C.   **The Identity of Persons in the Class Is Not Readily Available from Other Sources**

With respect to the third and final requirement set forth in Section 7609(f)(3), the information sought (and the identity of the persons with respect to whose tax liabilities the summonses have been issued) is not readily available to the Internal Revenue Service from other sources, but is available from _____.

Persons in the "John Doe" class may have filed tax returns with the Internal Revenue Service, but their names are unknown, and an inspection of a particular taxpayer's return is not likely to reveal understatements or misstatements of income resulting from _____. Their names cannot be obtained from _____.

Accordingly, the requirements for service of the "John Doe" summons have been satisfied in this proceeding.

II.   Courts Have Approved Prior "John Doe" Summonses in this Investigation

In _____ similar proceedings, Courts have approved the issuance of "John Doe" summonses pertaining to United States taxpayers who _____.

[add description of similar John Doe summonses authorized by courts]

III.   CONCLUSION

The summons for which the government seeks authorization meets the requirements of a "John Doe" summons. Accordingly, the Court should enter an order granting the Internal Revenue Service leave to serve a "John Doe" summons upon _____ in substantially the form as attached to the Exhibits Appendix to the Declaration of Revenue Agent _____ at Tab 1.

_____
United States Attorney

By: _____

Trial Attorney, Tax Division
U.S. Department of Justice

UNITED STATES DISTRICT COURT
_____ DISTRICT OF _____
_____ DIVISION

IN THE MATTER OF THE TAX
LIABILITIES OF:

JOHN DOES, United States taxpayers who,
during [*tax period and identify group*]

ORDER

THIS MATTER is before the Court upon the United States of America's EX PARTE

PETITION FOR LEAVE TO SERVE JOHN DOE SUMMONS. Based upon a review of the PETITION and

exhibits thereto, the Court has determined that the "John Doe" summons to

_____ and its affiliates and subsidiaries relates to the investigation of an

ascertainable group or class of persons, that there is a reasonable basis for believing that such

group or class of persons may fail or may have failed to comply with any provision of any

internal revenue law, and that the information sought to be obtained from the examination of the

records or testimony (and the identities of the persons with respect to whose liability the

summons is issued) are not readily available from other sources. It is therefore

ORDERED AND ADJUDGED that the Internal Revenue Service, through Revenue

Agent _____ or any other authorized officer or agent, may serve an

Internal Revenue Service "John Doe" summons upon _____ [and its affiliates and

subsidiaries] in substantially the form as attached to the Exhibits Appendix to the Declaration of

Revenue Agent _____at Tab 1. A copy of this Order shall be served together with the

summons.

DONE AND ORDERED this _____ day of _____, _____.

_____

UNITED STATES DISTRICT JUDGE

Copies furnished to:

_____

Trial Attorney, Tax Division
U.S. Department of Justice

_____

United States Attorney

UNITED STATES DISTRICT COURT
_____ DISTRICT OF _____
_____ DIVISION

IN THE MATTER OF THE TAX
LIABILITIES OF:

JOHN DOES, United States taxpayers who,
during [*tax period and identify group*]

NOTICE OF FILING *EX PARTE* PETITION
FOR LEAVE TO SERVE "JOHN DOE" SUMMONS

The United States of America notifies the Court that it has commenced this *ex parte*

proceeding pursuant to Section 7609(f) of the Internal Revenue Code (26 U.S.C.), for leave to

serve an Internal Revenue Service "John Doe" summons upon _____.

Pursuant to 26 U.S.C. § 7609(h), the determination to be made by the Court "shall be made *ex*

parte and shall be made solely on the petition and supporting affidavits." Thus, the pleadings

filed in this proceeding will not be served upon any person or entity and no other filings are

permitted from other persons or entities. Accordingly, this matter is ripe for the Court's

consideration. The United States requests that the Court review the Petition and supporting

documents and enter the proposed Order at the Court's earliest opportunity.

_____
United States Attorney

By: _____
Trial Attorney, Tax Division
U.S. Department of Justice

www.ingramcontent.com/pod-product-compliance
Lightning Source LLC
Chambersburg PA
CBHW080256180526
45167CB00006B/2550